who hates oppression and sows empowerment with every word he teaches."

—Andrew Vachss

"*The Confidence Course* is a gift to readers who hunger for hope and self-confidence. They will find, as I did, solutions to seemingly impossible problems drawn from Anderson's struggles to overcome fear and conquer anger and stress. And they will encounter the transforming power behind the author's enormous success."

—Fulton Oursler, Jr., Editor, Guideposts

"Walter Anderson believes in people and knows how to help them help themselves. Read this book and you'll have him cheering for you."

—Andrew Tobias

"Walter Anderson is a wonderful storyteller with a message that gets to everybody—about anger, about shyness, about how to wage the inner wars."

—David Lawrence, Publisher and Chairman, Miami Herald

"Walter is an extraordinary person whose sensitivity to the human issues of living is captivating. *The Confidence Course* speaks a truth that is elegant in its simplicity and deadly accurate in its scope and range. There are very few people who would not be enhanced by taking Walter's words to heart."

—Terry M. Giles, Chairman, Giles Enterprises

THE
CONFIDENCE
COURSE®

Also by Walter Anderson

Read with Me
The Greatest Risk of All
Courage Is a Three-Letter Word

THE CONFIDENCE COURSE®

SEVEN STEPS TO SELF-FULFILLMENT

WALTER ANDERSON

HarperPerennial

A Division of HarperCollins*Publishers*

The Confidence Course is a registered trademark belonging to Walter Anderson.

A hardcover edition of this book was published in 1997 by Harper-Collins Publishers.

THE CONFIDENCE COURSE®. Copyright © 1997 by Walter Anderson. All rights reserved. Printed in the United States of America. No part of this book may be used or reproduced in any manner whatsoever without written permission except in the case of brief quotations embodied in critical articles and reviews. For information address HarperCollins Publishers, Inc., 10 East 53rd Street, New York, NY 10022.

HarperCollins books may be purchased for educational, business, or sales promotional use. For information please write: Special Markets Department, HarperCollins Publishers, Inc., 10 East 53rd Street, New York, NY 10022.

First HarperPerennial edition published 1998.

Designed by Joseph Rutt

The Library of Congress has catalogued the hardcover edition as follows:

Anderson, Walter, 1944–
    The confidence course : seven steps to self-fulfillment / Walter Anderson. — 1st ed.
        p.   cm.
    ISBN 0-06-018729-8
    1. Self-confidence. 2. Stress (Psychology) 3. Success—Psychological aspects. I. Title
    BF575.S39A53   1997
    158'.1—dc20   96-31273

ISBN 0-06-109453-6 (pbk.)

01 02 ❖/RRD 10 9 8

For Eric and Melinda,
who have been loved by their mother and me
every day of their lives

CONTENTS

Seven Steps to Self-Fulfillment ix

Prologue: My Most Humiliating Moment 1

Introduction: We Can Learn to Be Confident 7

1 Who I Am 13

2 Never Say "Try" 25

3 How to Worry Well 31

4 How to Start a Conversation 39

5 What I Am, What I Have, What I Seem to Be 51

6 How to Overcome Shyness 71

7 How to Handle Mistakes: "SLIP" and "RIP" 75

8 How to Tell a Story 89

9 How to Use a Story 107

10 Why Am I So Angry? 117

11 Moving Beyond Anger 125

12 How to Love—and Be Loved 139

13 The Abuse of Love 151

14 Change Your Behavior—and Your Attitude Will Change 157

15 How to Handle Criticism 173

16 How to Take Risks 179

17 How to Find Courage 191

18 How to Give a Great Talk 199

19 How to Choose the Life You Want 215

20 What Matters Most? 225

Epilogue: My Most Rewarding Moment 229

List of Lists 233

List of Challenges 235

Author's Note 237

SEVEN STEPS TO SELF-FULFILLMENT

1. **Know who is responsible.**
   Accept personal responsibility for your behavior. When you say, "I am responsible," you can build a new life, even a new world.

2. **Believe in something big.**
   Your life is worth a noble motive.

3. **Practice tolerance.**
   You will like yourself a lot more, and so will others.

4. **Be brave.**
   Remember, courage is acting *with* fear, not without it. If the challenge is important to you, you're supposed to be nervous.

5. **Love someone.**
   Because you should know joy.

6. **Be ambitious.**
   No single effort will solve all of your problems, achieve all of your dreams, or even be enough. To want to be more than we are is real and normal and healthy.

7. **Smile.**
   Because no one else can do this for you.

THE
CONFIDENCE
COURSE®

My Most Humiliating Moment

Nothing can arouse anticipation more quickly in nearly everyone I know than a simple request: "Will you stand up before our group?" My most vivid memory of this kind of fear goes all the way back to my seventh-grade class at Immanuel Lutheran School in Mount Vernon, New York. This is a story I originally told in 1986 in my first book, *Courage Is a Three-Letter Word*, but it has a different—and happier—ending in this book.

I had turned thirteen only a few months before, and I believed all eyes were on me, burning right through the back of my neck as surely as if they were spotlights. I wanted to scream or cry or die. My heart beat so loudly in my ears, I was sure that others nearby could hear it too. As I look back over my life, despite thousands of other mistakes and embarrassments, this was my most humiliating moment.

Our teacher had ordered me to remove my shirt and stand at my desk. What bothered him was that I had my shirt collar up—a style worn by adolescents in the 1950s. He was going to make me an example before my classmates.

"Take off your shirt!" he ordered.

I promised not to wear my collar up again.

"I've caught you twice," he said, striding to my desk. "Take it off!"

He had me, and he knew it. Mount Vernon—four square miles of nearly seventy thousand people living just beyond the Bronx, the northernmost borough of New York City—is a town with a tear in its belly, a railroad cut right down its middle. I lived deep in the south side of town in a tenement on a street where kids often wore motorcycle jackets, greased their hair, talked hard, and tried to look unafraid—a neighborhood where the corner, however violent, was safer than the explosive tension at home. My home. Immanuel was deep in the north side—the "right side" of the tracks—in a section called Fleetwood. It might just as easily have been halfway across the world. It had prosperity, and it had peace. I crossed the tracks to go home every night, home to a block where kids wore their collars up.

"Take it off!" the teacher ordered again, hovering over me.

He was a tall man, and his body blocked any chance I might have had to run. Somebody giggled.

"Please . . ." I pleaded.

"Now!"

I unbuttoned the front of my shirt.

"Hurry up!"

I opened my cuffs and slipped the shirt off, draping it behind me on my chair. My undershirt had holes in it. Several people giggled.

"Stand up!"

I stood up.

The teacher, who had been standing beside my desk, marched back to the front of the classroom. He had been bullying me all year. I thought then—and I understand now—that it was because I was different, or at least seemed different. My clothes were unlike what the other students wore; mine were familiar in my neighborhood but unfamiliar in that school. Having forgotten to turn my collar down, I had given the teacher what he had been looking for.

I stood alone.

"Turn to page . . ." he said, ignoring me.

I heard my heart beat louder in my ears; the heat at the base of my neck was becoming unbearable. For a thirteen-year-old boy, his worst secret had been revealed. The undershirt with its holes for all to see proved I was poor, proved I was a south-sider, unworthy of the north-siders in the classroom.

Maybe it was seconds, maybe it was minutes before I reached for my shirt. It seemed like a lifetime.

"I didn't tell you to move," the teacher said from the front of the class.

I ignored him as I buttoned my shirt and sat down. The bell rang for recess before he got to me.

"Wait!" he ordered. Everyone stopped.

"Just Walter," he amended.

One or two students hesitated by the door, hoping to hear what he was going to say. "Move," he told them.

"You are going to learn to listen to me," he said. I was silent.

"Go to recess."

I walked to the door, turned back to the teacher, and called out his name.

"Yes?"

"Why don't you go to hell," I said, my eyes filling with tears.

From the depths of my anxiety, I had found the right response. It was not my words—which, because of the provocation, were deliberately disrespectful. It was that I had asserted myself. In that moment I had discovered the roots of my own dignity. I had dared to be myself. My mother, though she certainly did not condone my behavior, understood it and stood by me when I was threatened with expulsion. The following night, she pleaded with the school board to allow me to remain as a student until June. Then, she promised the members who patiently heard her plea, she would transfer me elsewhere.

"Anywhere," she was advised.

Vindicated, the teacher, for the most part, stopped the bullying; I quietly finished the school year.

*   *   *

I met Dr. Norman Vincent Peale when *Courage Is a Three-Letter Word* was published. Three years later, well after we had become friends, he asked me to write an article on forgiveness for his magazine, *Guideposts*. The piece, which appeared in November 1989, was titled "My Toughest Struggle." I described how, as an adult, I had learned to understand my father's alcoholism and thus was able, finally, to control the anger that had raged within me for years.

I received many letters as a result of that article, but there was one that touched me more than all the others:

"Dear Walter," it began . . .

> *I'm really sorry I made you take off your shirt and embarrassed you in front of the class. I had forgotten all about it until I read it in your book this morning, and, oh, how ashamed I am that I did something like that— especially since I was there to teach you and the other young people love.*

It turned out, he wrote, that his wife had read the article in *Guideposts* and suspected that I was the same Walter Anderson who had been in his class at Immanuel three decades earlier. When he visited the local library the next morning, he found a copy of *Courage Is a Three-Letter Word*, and he discovered the passage that described what had occurred between us. He explained in his letter how, when he was a boy, he was picked on repeatedly and mercilessly by street toughs, and how this bullying had left a painful impression on him:

Walter, I was at least as afraid of you as you were of me. I thought you were the Dead End Kids and Blackboard Jungle *all rolled into one. Who knows how much your inner self saw me as your threatening father, and how much my inner self saw you as the bullies who terrified me as a child? I'm so sorry things weren't different, and I know that as the adult it was up to me to set the example.*

To help me understand his state of mind at the time, he wrote about terrible hardships he, his wife, and his family had endured. And he expressed a wish: "I hope and pray that you forgive me."

I had forgiven him, of course . . . years ago. First, however, I had to grow from an angry adolescent into a confident adult. The journey was sometimes painful—but isn't life all about ups *and* downs, and about learning from both?

So is *The Confidence Course.*

By the time you reach the Epilogue and read my response to the letter from this teacher who changed my life in more ways than he knew, I hope that *you* will have grown as well on your journey through *The Confidence Course.*

6

INTRODUCTION

We Can Learn to Be Confident

There I stood—alone, trembling, hidden in the wings of Ford's Theatre in Washington, D.C. Over the loudspeakers a cultured male voice warmly welcomed the audience, reminding all that the use of cameras and electronic devices was strictly prohibited.

With each passing second, my pulse climbed a notch higher. There was no escape; it was too late to turn back or run away. Hundreds of people were out there, waiting. I knew that in only a few minutes I would have to leave the security of the heavy drapes that now hid me from view, walk to the center of this historic stage, and begin a one-man show, a ninety-minute performance I had written called Talkin' Stuff.

I shook my head. "How," I wondered, "did I get

myself into this fix? What have I done? Why, oh why, am I here?"

Years ago I heard a fellow remark, "There are no happy endings." He's almost right, I thought. He should have added, "There's only struggle." Life is unfair, and it's sometimes tragic. The other guy gets to pick the fruit from the tree we plant, gets the reward that should have been ours, steals the credit for our work. We see lazy people get lucky and very bad things happen to the very nicest of people. Our own families and friends at times disappoint or even hurt us. And we hurt and disappoint them. No, life is not fair.

So, knowing that I may get kicked in the rump anyway, despite giving my best and most sincere effort, how can I possibly face the future with confidence?

By being one hundred percent alive.

That's exactly what the late Dr. Norman Vincent Peale, who was my friend, told me when I asked him that question several years ago, and I've yet to hear a better answer.

"Be one hundred percent alive."

Do it. Commit. Commit yourself to this book. You're reading this because you want to live with greater confidence right now. You hope to discover something in these pages that will strengthen your resolve, boost your courage, reduce your anxieties and fears, maybe even help you to answer for yourself: *Who am I? What do I want to do?* And you'd like to feel competent, fulfilled, needed. And, yes, you want to love.

Okay, you say. I'm ready. How do I begin?

First, the catch. No book—including this one—can do the job for you. The truth is, I cannot make you confident. What I *can* do is show you how to make yourself *more* confident. So, if you don't quit right now, I'll make this promise to you: Stick with this course—and it *is* a course—and you'll get the best I've got to give. No tricks, no empty pledges. You'll learn what I know works.

This book grew out of a seven-week course on self-confidence that I was encouraged to create and teach at the New School for Social Research in New York City in 1994. Elizabeth Dickey, the dean, and Marjorie Vai, the department chair, were persuasive, assuring me that a genuine need existed. The class would be held, we agreed, if it could attract ten to twelve students—a reasonable expectation for a new course. Three weeks before registration concluded, however, Professor Vai called to alert me that, although classes normally were "capped" at twenty students, more students were signing up. She asked how I felt about a larger class size. "The more the merrier," I replied. Twenty-five students seemed a reasonable forecast at that point. It was clear that she and Dean Dickey had been right about the need: If more than twenty students signed up, it indicated genuine interest. They were more right than we knew. By the first class, fifty-four students had enrolled, and we moved from a classroom to an amphitheater. Additionally, the editor of *Self* magazine at the time, Alexandra Penney, heard about the class and assigned a reporter, Lauren Picker, to become one of my students. Lauren wrote an article about the course, which was published in the March 1995 issue of *Self.*

Afterward, Alexandra Penney told me why she felt that *The Confidence Course* was more valuable than other similar attempts: "It is real. No psychobabble. You share practical, insightful advice based on real-life experience. This touches people—and it works. It is not the usual 'feel-good' counseling that doesn't last."

Where does *The Confidence Course* come from?

First, from my own life experiences and from those of the hundreds of eminently successful people I've come to know well over the last three decades.

I've learned that an individual may be supremely confident in one area of life but be a "basket case" in another. For example, a successful stockbroker who trades millions of shares a day with confidence may shake at the thought of addressing a room full of shareholders.

As for myself, I've lived with fear and anxiety all my life. I cannot remember *not* having to struggle against the most painful feelings of inferiority. As the child of a violent alcoholic father, living in a tenement, I felt vulnerable as a boy and feared being hurt or, worse, embarrassed. As an adult, I grew so sensitive to this subject that when I wrote my first book, *Courage Is a Three-Letter Word*, I titled its first chapter "What Will I Do When They Find Out I'm Me?"

I suffer anxiety attacks to this day. Nevertheless, despite my nervousness, I accept many of the hundreds of requests I receive to speak before groups of all sizes. I have been a guest on national radio and television talk shows, and I have been the host of a live television special and a TV series encouraging children and parents to read together. I've been interviewed by radio, television, magazine, and newspaper reporters. I've written scores of articles and four books. I've edited the world's largest-circulation magazine, *Parade*, for more than fifteen years. And, as the opening of this passage describes, I've performed onstage, alone.

What have I learned?

I've learned to speak and write clearly, effectively, and, most important, with confidence—*no matter how chicken I feel*. I believe human beings can transform themselves, and I know that real confidence comes only from experience. Thus, you'll learn in *The Confidence Course* what I've learned, in language that's direct: *How to worry well*. That's right, worry *well*—which is to discover how to harness your anxiety and diminish your aching feelings of inferiority.

How to say what you mean.

How to persuade.

How to tell a story well.

How to hold another person's attention.

How to inspire others to like and respect you.

How to really gain from your mistakes.

How to recognize and appreciate the significant difference between being loved and loving.

How to define genuine success, live with dignity, and live with meaning.

How to find the courage you need when you need it— those times, for example, when you have to say "no" to someone or when you are asked to stand up to speak before a group.

How to remember things.

And what to do with your hands, your feet, even your lips.

Let's start with your fingers. Turn the page.

1

Who I Am

You made the right decision.

By taking the risk to be here, to be with me on this page, you've taken the first step toward greater confidence. You'll find the information in this workbook to be direct, easy to understand, and effective. Yes, this stuff really does work. In fact, if you read only through the third chapter, absorb only its message, and take on only the challenge at its conclusion, I know you'll not only enjoy the results—you'll also grow in confidence. Welcome to *The Confidence Course*.

> *Okay, I'm here. I turned the page.*
> *Now, why will I be more confident?*

The Confidence Course, anchored in practical life experience, will work for you because we *can* transform ourselves.

The truth is, you and I define who we are every day by the choices we make, and thus we choose who we want to be. I create myself. So do you. I invent myself. You do too. You and I are not what we eat; we are what we *think*. Confidence, by definition, is an attitude—and your attitude toward people and situations, just like mine, is subject to change. You're going to learn here how to swap one set of perceptions for another. The world will remain the same; how you *see* the world will be different.

When do we start?

Right now. Here's what you need to know about *The Confidence Course* to get the most out of it: The course is a personal workbook. It is taken and developed from what I believe to be the most practical and useful material in articles and books I've written, talks I've given across the country, and, of course, *The Confidence Course* classes themselves that I've taught as a member of the faculty of the New School for Social Research in New York City.

You'll see that, as you work at the course, your confidence will grow. So read and attempt everything. Mark up and fold down the pages. The more wrinkles in the seams, the greater this book's value. Write in the margins, highlight paragraphs and points. It is your life that makes this book come alive. Without you, these are merely words on paper. Truly, it is you who will give this book its life. I may be the guide, but the adventure is yours.

Now, here are some details about *The Confidence*

Course you should find useful: The book explores questions that occasionally trouble all of us about competition, mistakes, courage, failure, loss and tragedy, risk-taking, relationships, noble motives, and love. It contains, among other things, practical advice on how to structure a talk, tell a story dramatically, give an unforgettable introduction . . .

But this is not a book about public speaking—it's a book about personal confidence. We need to recognize, though, that the dread of being asked to speak before a group is, as many national surveys indicate, the number one fear among a majority of adults. *The Confidence Course* thus describes how to master this painful anxiety—and how to use your body, your voice, and the stage itself to achieve "presence."

So how does public speaking relate to personal confidence?

Normal people feel real terror when asked to stand up and speak before a group. More than being merely acknowledged, such an obvious and often-discussed fear must be welcomed in a course about confidence. We have much to learn from this particular anxiety, even if we never speak at a podium. Because, when you think about it, don't we speak publicly most of the time? Just as we're all salesmen, so too each of us routinely is a public speaker. The two are related. We sell to ourselves every time we decide that we can or cannot do something. In fact, have you ever noticed how amazingly persuasive you are with yourself—particularly when it comes to the cannots? This has a lot to do with communicating.

As Henry Ford suggested: *Whether you say you can or whether you say you cannot, you are right.* You regularly communicate with yourself, and in nearly every contact with another human being, you are either a speaker or a listener. In other words, you're almost always communicating. Would you like to be better at it?

You can be. So can I.

The power of words certainly is not limited to the podium or the stage. Even the most popular performers on earth spend only a tiny fraction of their time before an audience. Each of us observes—and is observed—every day. We need and are affected by other people, whether it's the cashier at the checkout counter, a boss, a client, a surgeon, a lover, a teacher, a friend . . . the list is endless.

To help understand and face our daily challenges, *The Confidence Course* is a guide to reaching the peak—which is how to give a talk and perform more effectively before others. But, more, it maps the mountain itself, illustrating how to communicate better and with more confidence in normal life situations, whether your goal is simply to feel better about yourself or to conclude a personal or business relationship. It's about dealing with real-life fear and real-life joy, sadness, and disappointment. And it's about triumph. What every one of my students learns, finally, is that performing before an audience is merely strutting our best, our most practiced, stuff. I once complimented the actor Gregory Peck on the brilliance of an off-the-cuff comment he had made. He replied candidly, "My best extemporane-ous remarks are those I've rehearsed the most."

Keep in mind that your goal in *The Confidence Course* is to learn to climb the mountain of your choice—and to enjoy the trek as well.

You'll find it useful to read about the experiences of successful people—some famous, some not—that appear throughout the book. You'll also find "One-Minute Stories," which are provided as examples to help you improve your own storytelling, but also are often inspiring. And, finally, throughout *The Confidence Course* you'll read actual questions that I've received from students, like this one:

If, as you said, I can create the person
I'd like to be, how do I start?

Say, "I am responsible," and accept personal responsibility for your own life. This is the first—and most important—of the Seven Steps to Self-Fulfillment:

THE FIRST STEP TO SELF-FULFILLMENT

1. Know who is responsible.
   Accept personal responsibility for your behavior. When you say, "I am responsible," you can build a new life, even a new world.

Theologians and philosophers have observed and preached for centuries the simple truth that destiny is not something that happens to you, not something you wait for: Destiny is a choice, *your* choice. You choose the life you lead. Each of us has the capacity to make happiness happen.

But my circumstances are terrible!

Look, I can hold your hand, share a good cry, commiserate, tell you that I know life is not fair, that you got dealt a crummy hand, that you've been cheated by things outside your control, that the ill which has befallen you is not your fault. I can say with conviction that I understand and sympathize with the fact that we cannot prevent all of the disappointments, losses, and tragedies that occur in our lives, and I realize that we are not born with equal abilities. We agree, life can sting.

So where does that leave us? Right where we began, with the first of the Seven Steps to Self-Fulfillment: Know who is responsible. *I am responsible.* Although I may not be able to prevent the worst from happening, I am responsible for my attitude toward the inevitable misfortunes that darken life. Bad things do happen; how I respond to them defines my character and the quality of my life.

I can choose to sit in perpetual sadness, immobilized by the gravity of my loss, or I can choose to rise from the pain and treasure the most precious gift I have—life itself.

You and I are human beings, infinitely capable of change. You can lead a fuller, richer life. When—finally and with no excuses—you accept responsibility for your own life, you not only gain incredible power to achieve positive goals and be more confident, but you also are able to diminish the pain that inevitably accompanies an emotional wound.

To fully accept responsibility, though, we need to understand who we *really* are. Have you ever asked yourself, "Who am I?"

Three factors determine who you are: heredity, environment, and, most important, your responses to both.

You are the only you who will ever live. In front of a mirror or in front of a microphone, you are who you are, and accepting this plain truth can be both the toughest and the most rewarding challenge of your life.

There has never been anyone quite like you, or me.

I once asked my friend Dr. Carl Sagan, the distinguished scientist and scholar, to calculate the chances of a particular individual being born:

"One thing to consider," he advised, "is how many spermatozoa exist in a single ejaculation. Let's say it's three hundred million. That's three hundred million *possible* human beings. Next there are questions of the physiology of both parents—and timing. The three hundred million spermatozoa represent only one sexual act at a particular time."

The arithmetic helps us to understand just how special we are. Imagine more than three hundred million chances to be you! Consider that your mother had three hundred million chances to be precisely who she was, that your father had another three hundred million. It could be argued that the odds against your being born are 300,000,000 multiplied by 300,000,000 multiplied by 300,000,000 multiplied by whatever the chances would be that your folks would meet in the first place and create you when they did. You are indeed a long shot, my friend—the winner, the day you're born, against odds of billions to one. You *are* unique!

Now, let's take this a step further: Is it our genes (or our chromosomes or some chemical factor) that determines who we are? Only partly. With heredity, our uniqueness merely begins. Heredity—all those genetic combinations that tell our cells to produce brown or blue eyes, curly or straight hair, and that predispose us to and sometimes immunize us against certain ailments or diseases—is like the car we drive.

Road conditions and weather are the environment. The car may be capable of speeding one hundred miles per hour on a bright, sunny day along a freshly blacktopped highway; but change the environment to a muddy logging trail at night during a hurricane, and the car may not move at all.

Heredity dictates how high we can jump under perfect conditions. It determines how much information we can possibly absorb and retain, how tall we can possibly be, how fast we can possibly run. Heredity is our potential, but environment is our opportunity. If you were genetically capable of being the greatest long-distance swimmer who ever lived but, unfortunately, you were born two centuries ago to an Eskimo family in the northern reaches, it's a safe bet that you would never achieve your potential as a swimmer. You would lack both the opportunity and the environment.

If heredity is the car and environment is the condition of the road, then you are the driver. It is you, more than any other factor, that decides the speed and safety of that car.

Who you are evolves from the potential you've inherited, the opportunities you receive, and the choices you make. The final factor—your response to heredity and environment—is more profoundly important to you than the arithmetic of 300,000,000 multiplied by 300,000,000 multiplied by 300,000,000. It is your choices that make you uniquely you.

We are handed our heredity with no apologies, and our environment is often beyond our control. We have the power, though, to face life, to make choices, and, most important, to hope. A stroke may render a woman helpless, but it is hope—true hope—that moves her to stretch, to test her muscles, to learn to speak again.

True hope dwells on the possible, even when life seems to be a plot written by someone who wants to see how much adversity we can overcome.

True hope responds to the real world, to real life; it is an active effort.

False hope, on the other hand, is dangerous; it is pathological. False hope is the cancer patient denying his illness; true hope recognizes the disease and seeks to conquer it or cope with it.

True hope reminds us that each of us is the driver of his own car, that we are not helpless behind the wheel.

I can speak with conviction because I feel this deeply. As I said, I grew up on the south side of town in Mount Vernon, New York. I remember one night when my mother asked me to walk to the telephone booth across the street from our tenement to make a call to my older brother. I was fourteen. We had no telephone at the time.

I can't remember the message or our discussion, but I clearly recall the incident because, when I replaced the receiver, I noticed blood on my hand. I touched my face with the other hand and found more blood.

I wasn't bleeding, but whoever had used the phone before me had been hurt or wounded, which was not unusual in the neighborhood in which I was raised. Opening up the glass bifold doors, I looked to one side and then to the other. I ran across the street, bounded up the stairs to the door of our railroad flat, nervously opened it, stepped inside and up to the kitchen sink, and washed the blood from my face before my mother could see it.

About an hour later, I sat alone on the front stoop and wondered about the mysterious person whose blood had covered my face.

Then I became angry.

I'm getting out of here, I promised myself. And, for the first time that I can remember, I meant it.

There's an often-told story in the Far East about the Chinese grandfather who, each day of his life, rose early, climbed to the top of a nearby hill that blocked the early-morning sunlight, picked up a pebble, walked back down the hill, and dropped the pebble on the other side of a stream near his home. His son and grandson joined him in this task. "Why do we do this?" the grandson finally asked.

"As long as you continue to do this and teach your children and grandchildren to carry the pebbles," the grandfather promised, "we're going to move this hill." The boy persisted, "But, Grandfather, you'll never see the hill moved."

The old man nodded and replied: "Yes, but I know that someday it will be moved."

CHALLENGE NO. 1: TRUE HOPE

The spirit of *The Confidence Course* is true hope: the certain knowledge that you and I are not helpless; that you can, when you set your mind to it, move a hill—or a mountain—of doubt. Gaining confidence, like living with true hope, is a conscious, *active* effort.

So, during the next seven days, pay attention to all examples you observe of true hope versus false hope, the little incidents as well as the big ones. You may be surprised to discover how many instances you note.

Keep a list. Examine the examples you've gathered at the end of the week. Include in your analysis these questions:

• **Do others respond in the same way to the person**

who lives with true hope and to the person who lives with false hope?

• In each case of true hope or false hope, what does the person involved seem to be focusing on?

Remember to save the list. We're going to examine these results further.

2

Never Say "Try"

Alone among the creatures of the earth, human beings can explore the question, "Why?" Although animals send signals, they're unable to use words to refine their messages. The cry of a bear cub, for example, will summon his mother; a bee tail-dances an alarm, and the hive responds. Neither bees nor bear cubs, though, can communicate what is troubling them. Only when Mother Bear arrives on the scene can she discover what has frightened Junior: Is the quill of a porcupine stuck in his paw? Is he caught in a steel trap? Is some unfamiliar, strange-smelling creature—a human being, perhaps—threatening? Similarly, bees buzz from their hive, ready to attack without question, to willingly surrender their lives when one bee, not even a leader, signals danger. But, like Mother Bear, until they arrive, the bees do not know the character or size of the problem.

You, on the other hand, can make a telephone call to the other side of the planet, describe a medical emergency, and receive instant, helpful guidance from doctors thousands of miles away. You can order a lamp from a catalog and never see the person who made it or the person who sent it to you. You can describe in detail a concern of yours to the police or to firefighters before they're even dispatched to your home. If you hear a child scream, immediately your heart beats faster, the adrenaline pumps. But if the scream is followed by the words "My doll fell behind the couch," you rest easier and maybe even smile.

Your ability to acquire and to use a growing vocabulary is a biological and social gift invisibly endowed across the centuries, from the very dawn of humankind. The first cave dwellers needed words as much in their time as you do today because, compared to other living creatures, our ancient ancestors were in many ways ill-equipped for survival. Their fragile hides could tear easily, thus exposing their internal organs to injury. Unlike lizards and fish, our distant relatives needed to clothe themselves for warmth. A few degrees' drop in body temperature, and they, like you, could fall sick and maybe perish. A common ant had more suitable armor; birds had better eyesight; rodents had superior hearing. The claws and hoofs of human beings, compared to those of other tenants of the planet, were delicate and dull, barely adequate tools for digging in the hard earth, climbing sharp ledges, or discouraging predators.

With such seemingly pathetic equipment, how could human beings possibly survive?

They had words.

Like us, they could talk to each other. They could organize searches for food and shelter and plan defense systems. They could describe things. Words made it possible to pass on knowledge to others and to succeeding generations, to improve and to enlarge inventions and tools, to communicate a range of emotions, including love and hate. The late Benjamin Lee Whorf, a pioneer in the study of linguistics, once observed that our human ability to learn language allows each of us, first, to communicate with someone else; second, to think, which is to communicate with ourselves; and third, to acquire the attitudes that shape our whole outlook on life.

To gain greater confidence, it helps to understand this incredible ability of ours to learn words—because *confidence is an attitude*. And, as Whorf observed, we *acquire* our attitudes.

Are you saying that by changing my words I can change my attitude?

Yes, that's a good place for personal growth to begin. You are what you *think*—and you, like me, think in language. For example, you think: "I cannot speak before the class." Said as such, the "not" is a monster declaration: I can*not*.

Yes, but what if I really cannot?

There's a possibility that you are saying—thinking—something that simply is not accurate. Let's take another look at your words: "I cannot speak before the class."

The sentence is firm and final, isn't it? You mean what you say, that's for sure. Some of your fellow students would even argue that your statement is completely honest and that I should accept your judgment. Okay, I respect your choice, because it is yours to make. What you might consider, though, is that your statement is accurate only in its power to self-fulfill. I agree that as long as you say with such conviction that you cannot speak before the class, you will not speak before the class—and no one, least of all me, is going to make you. You cannot.

Imagine, though, if you said instead: "I have not been able to speak before the class."

Now, that's indisputable. I totally agree. It is a perfectly accurate and truthful thought. Most important, it does not slam the door shut on your future choices. Actually, it enlarges your vision, doesn't it? It respects your ability to master—if not today, then tomorrow—whatever you need to learn in order to speak before the class. This statement does not imply, as does the first, that you believe you will *never* be ready to speak before the class—which, bluntly, is true only if you make it so.

One day, when I was a young Marine stationed at Camp Lejeune in North Carolina, my hands were crushed in an accident. The doctors had to wait a few days for the swelling to subside before they were able to discover whether I had movement or feeling in my fingers. My platoon sergeant joined them for the test.

"Try to move the first finger of your right hand," the doctor instructed me.

As he suggested, I tried, but nothing happened.

"I can't," I told him, and he said we'd try again tomorrow.

"Wait just a minute," the sergeant interrupted. "Move the first finger of your right hand now!"

I struggled. The finger moved.

I've thought of that experience occasionally over the years whenever, from time to time, I've heard myself or someone else promise to *try* to achieve a goal. This word should carry a warning label:

> ## WARNING:
> Authorities warn that "try" is a dangerous expression that has enormous power to influence your behavior. It's toxic. Use it very carefully. When "try" creeps into your language or into your thoughts, pluck it out quickly.

After all this time, I still fight the "try" bug myself. Sometimes I want to try when I really should *do*.

> ## CHALLENGE NO. 2: NOT TO TRY
> To feel the immense power of the word "try," consciously use it over the next few days whenever possible to direct others:

"Try to hand me that pencil."
"Try to give me that check."
"Try to pump me a full tank."
"Try to stand up."
"Try to sit down."
"Try to kiss me."
"Try to hand me that book."
"Try to turn the television off."

The possibilities are endless—and instructive. Expect a range of responses, from indifference to confusion to annoyance. Be prepared, though, to explain quickly—very quickly—that your use of the word "try" is part of a course you're taking.

After this exercise, you may find yourself using—and thinking—this particular word less frequently. At the very least, this should help you to grow more conscious of try's dangers.

As a second part of this assignment, listen carefully to the language of others over the next seven days, and when you hear an expression that limits a person's choices, as with "I cannot," jot it down. When you're alone, review the list and ask yourself the following questions:

Have I used the same expressions under similar circumstances?

How, precisely, do these particular words limit choice?

How could the people involved have amended or conveyed their thoughts both to be more accurate and to give themselves more choices?

3

How to Worry Well

At the Walter Reed Army Institute of Research in the 1950s, a laboratory experiment that is a classic in behavioral research was conducted using eight rhesus monkeys. The eight were divided into pairs. Each pair received periodic electric shocks, but one monkey in each pair was able— when a light flashed on—to prevent itself from being shocked by pressing a lever. The other monkey in each pair could not prevent itself from being shocked. The shocks continued regularly over some weeks. Four of the eight monkeys developed terrible stomach lesions and ulcers, and they died. The others showed no similar symptoms. Which monkeys got sick? The answer may surprise you. It was the four monkeys who were able to prevent electric shocks to themselves who got the ulcers and died.

*   *   *

Many Americans early in their lives acquire a contagious, crippling disease of inestimable pain—an illness of such potential severity that literally thousands upon thousands take their lives rather than try to find its cure. This dread disease is *worry*. It touches everyone.

How has it affected you?

It has made *me* miserable. Very little that I've done in my life has been so damaging and painful to me as my worrying about things that might happen. When I was a young adult, I thought that the people I admired somehow didn't worry as I did. So, because I was foolish enough to believe that the strong and the successful didn't worry, I pretended not to. I *acted* unconcerned. I might just as well have tried to cap a volcano. I was convinced that worrying was negative, unique to losers, and a sure sign of failure. What a stubborn mule I can be! There was no single enlightening event, no epiphany, no turning point for me. Instead, it took many years and scores of experiences, needless discomfort, and torment before I realized how wrong I was.

Because of my life's work as an editor and an author, I have had the wonderful opportunity to come to know many successful people, the very people I thought didn't worry as I did. Hundreds of times I've found myself looking into their eyes and asking the question that has caused me more worry than any other, the question that has haunted me since I was a teenager: "*When it is dark and you are alone, do you ever say to yourself, 'What will I do when they find out I'm me?'*"

Now here's the thing: I've never failed to make a friend with that question. And I've never failed to get a nod. It was as if I knew who they were. I understood. And because I understood, I could be trusted. I've seen it melt the cool, disciplined, practiced composure of some of the planet's most prominent leaders—and that includes executives in charge of global companies, respected clergy, scientists, educators, entertainers, authors, artists, and athletes.

I discovered that they were like the rest of us. They were like me! And what was it I had been afraid—and in many ways still am—that others might discover?

EVERYONE'S FEARS

I'm afraid that I am inferior.
I'm afraid that I am vulnerable.
I'm afraid that I deserve to be rejected.

How about you? When it's dark and you're alone in your most troubled moments, do you worry that someone will find out that you're not quite good enough, that you can be hurt, that maybe you don't belong? If so, read on. Your fears, my fears, are shared by millions of sane people. We are not alone. If the truth be told, it is we who are the majority, and it is we who are normal. In fact, fear itself, once you understand it, can be okay. It can save your life.

Fear, though, is not anxiety. Anxiety is something else—and, for our confidence to grow, we need to clearly understand the difference between the two.

Fear is what kept our primitive ancestors alive in a hostile world. They had no time to wonder or ponder. They had a minute, maybe two, to make the life-or-death choice: "Should we fight or should we run?" Adrenaline flooded their bloodstreams, adding speed, energy, and strength. Their veins and arteries constricted simultaneously to slow the bleeding if they were wounded. Their pulses quickened, their bodily defenses stiffened. This physical response to a clear and present danger was fear—the same fear we depend on to save our own lives.

Today, most of what we call "fear" is something else. It is *anxiety*, a response not to danger itself but to *anticipated* danger. The cave dweller was rightly concerned about being some creature's breakfast on the spot. What he felt was *real* fear. When we worry about something that might happen later—when we say, "I just know I'm going to fail!"—that's anxiety. When the brakes in your car stop working on a hill, what you feel is fear. When you worry over what you'll say at a meeting next Tuesday, that's anxiety—and anxiety is a lot more agonizing than fear.

Fear usually ends with the event: The car stops, the fear is over.

Anxiety, on the other hand, can be endless.

Why do I emphasize the distinction?

I do because your body often does not.

Have you ever noticed how your body reacts when you're anxious? Quickened pulse. Sweaty palms. Dry throat, just as if you were face-to-face with a creature who wanted to gobble you up for breakfast! Anxiety is so frustrating: all that energy, and nothing to do with it. You can't run or fight, because there's nothing to run from, nothing to fight. You sit with a knot in your stomach, anticipating danger.

From our own life experiences, as well as studies like the one with the rhesus monkeys at the Walter Reed Army Institute, we know that anxiety can produce symptoms ranging from mild discomfort to psychological and physical incapacitation or even death. On the other hand, we know that anxiety—as a real source of energy—can, when properly directed, help us to live better.

What I did not understand when I was younger was that worry, whether prompted by fear or anxiety, is an expression of nervous energy and, as such, is potentially helpful, healthy, and good. The greatest heroes, the most successful and triumphant people, worry. The difference is that they do something about it: They worry *well*.

Can I learn to do that?

Yes—and you'll learn more quickly if you keep in mind that it's only when our imagination fires blanks, when we exaggerate our fears, that worrying is unhealthy: "I start school Monday; *no one will like me*." "Thank you for the opportunity; *I know I'll fail*." I have imagined such outrageous consequences of everyday concerns (well, they *could* occur), and I now blush when I recall them. Not satisfied with merely sneaking into my son's bedroom when he was an infant to make sure he was breathing, sometimes I'd pinch him and tell my wife, "Honey, Eric's awake!"

To keep our worrying healthy—in other words, to worry well—we must learn to direct into productive channels the energy that fear and anxiety provide. That's accomplished in two steps:

TWO STEPS TO WORRYING WELL

1. **Understand what you fear.**
   More often than not, most of our worries begin to disappear when we analyze them—because it's hard to go on worrying when we begin to examine what troubles us, when we see our worries in context: "I can't sleep at night. I'm so terrified of failing the final exam Wednesday morning." Well, what's the worst thing that can happen? I mean the *worst*. You might also ask yourself: "Why do I think I may fail? Is there something obvious I can do to pass? Is this the first time I've had a similar concern?"

2. **Take action.**
   Nothing quells anxiety faster than action. Once we thoroughly examine our concerns, more often than not we find out what to do: "What can I do now to prepare for the future?" Often it takes a practical effort, like studying for an exam rather than worrying about it.

CHALLENGE NO. 3:
EVERY LITTLE WORRY

Do this experiment for a month.

It's an exercise that has worked wonders for me and nearly all of my students: Keep a diary and write down what worries you when it worries you. Whatever the worry, however small or large, log it. Every time you have a concern—even when it may seem like only seconds since the last one—write it down. If you have the same concern repeatedly, write it down repeatedly.

Share the results with no one. In every other aspect of *The Confidence Course*—including the first two challenges—I would encourage you, if you find it helpful, to discuss with others what you're learning. This exercise is the exception; this one you must live alone. If, after thirty days, you want to talk about it with friends, fine. But not before.

You may become as excited as others who've worked at this assignment in *The Confidence Course* because of what you'll discover fairly quickly—and, like many of them, you may find it equally hard to resist sharing the findings. Hang tough. Also, as I said, you'll begin to see results soon, and thus you may be tempted to cut the exercise short as insights emerge. Don't.

Do the entire month. I pledge to you that this exercise alone, when done with diligence and in silence, is worth it.

4

How to Start a Conversation

Everyone craves to belong. Like most other living things, we were not meant to live alone. Remember the simple amoeba, the one-celled creature every high school student studies? Separated from its group, it struggles to rejoin the others—just as we do. However complex our lives may seem, however we may feel an urge at times to deny or discount our need for other people, the truth is that being secure in the company of others—*to belong*—is important to everyone.

In the next several pages we're going to examine the nature of some of our relationships: how we've learned from our earliest years to hesitate, to be cautious, sometimes to behave like a child when we need most to be an adult; how and why we cling to false notions that cripple our ability to gain confidence; and, most important, how to shake ourselves free. We'll do this, first, by taking a close look at how we come to see ourselves—and how others come to see us. Then we'll work at affecting those perceptions—ours and theirs.

The first three chapters together contain the basic building materials we need to construct the architecture of a healthy, confident person; they are the foundation that supports the rest of the course. Now, let me wave a flag of caution: Sometimes you may feel inspired to rush to the next challenge when an assigned task moves you. If you get excited about a breakthrough you make in *The Confidence Course*—as some other students have—remember that it has taken years for you to grow into who you are. Consequently, it is wise to assume that it will take time to make the kind of changes in yourself that will stick.

If you were seated in a classroom as a student of *The Confidence Course*, the lessons would be taught one week apart over the course of seven weeks. So, please, slow down—and don't skip ahead. The challenge is not to see how fast you can complete the work I assign but how much you can gain from it. Don't gulp down the course; a bite at a time is best. Also, now that you've started your daily diary, undoubtedly you've made important discoveries about yourself and your worries, and you may be bursting to trumpet what you've learned. Again, resist—do not share your findings. Not yet. We've got more ground to cover first, like what's just ahead.

How we identify ourselves to one another ("My name is Walter Anderson, and I am an editor") is more often than not a recognition of our membership in certain groups—a family, a nationality, or whatever. Look at how much is in that simple declaration. How many groups might I be identified with? Does my name itself eliminate groups to which it's likely I do not belong? In which groups do my apparent nationality and my occupation most likely place me? Take the thought a step further: How much might be supposed about me? What would you suspect I believe about democracy, let's say, or capitalism? Whether you're right or wrong, in which groups do your answers place me?

All this from a simple declaration—and you haven't even heard my accent! Actually, even before we open our mouths and allow our languages and accents to reveal our backgrounds, our clothes already have reflected the groups we belong to. What we select to wear—or how we style our hair—announces who we are as loudly as a cymbal crash, because clothes and other elements of our appearance invite and encourage expectations.

If the President of the United States, for example, attended an economic conference dressed as flamboyantly as a rock star, how might he be received? If, on the other hand, a leader of the Harley Owners Group showed up at a motorcycle rally dressed like the President delivering a State of the Union address ... well, you get the idea. Understand, though, that what we infer—the behavior we expect—from someone's appearance can be wholly wrong. Clothes do not make the person; clothes, at best, are a clue (sometimes a misleading clue) that tells us where a person seems to belong.

CHALLENGE NO. 4: APPEARANCE

What do your clothes, your style of dress, and your personal hygiene say about you?

What expectations do you think they raise in others?

Are they the expectations you desire?

Clothes, style of dress, and personal hygiene frequently communicate more eloquently—and often more quickly—than language. What message does your appearance convey?

Tonight, take an inventory. Although we'll discuss appearance further, if you determine that a change is needed and you have the means, take action immediately.

Group influence is strong stuff. For any of us to grow in confidence, it helps to understand its power. To emphasize the point, consider that millions of lives have been lost in wars throughout history as humans defended the ideals of the groups to which they belonged. That craving—the need to belong, the urge to act as the group expects us to act—is a powerful instinct. Why do we feel these things? Where does this powerful need to belong come from? Is it possible that the answer may be locked away, hidden in our childhood memories? If so, *what's the most important lesson we learn when we are children*? Let's take a look:

The first group we belong to is especially important, and we usually don't recognize this at the time. Often composed of just two persons, it has been the source of endless legend and speculation: It is you and the person who cares for you as an infant.

At first you can't differentiate yourself from the world around you. Your body and the crib are not separate; the smiling face and warm breath you sometimes see and feel are not yours, but you don't know that yet. Then changes occur. You notice that when you move your head, the view is, well, different. Touching your foot and touching your face are not quite the same, but both are considerably different from touching someone else's hand. You learn that, by yourself, you can't will that smiling face and warm breath to appear. You need to communicate your desires—and, as any parent can attest, you do. You are no longer the sole inhabitant of your world. You have begun to perceive, to feel your need for others. Pleasure and discomfort are sensations that can depend on someone else. The first separation in our lives is our discovery somewhere in infancy that I and you are not the same. Our dependence on others grows; our sense of vulnerability grows equally, because we have learned we cannot control everything around us.

The quality of the relationship between "you" and "I" flavors the relationships that follow. We learn what we can influence; we learn whom we can trust—and, by taking risks, our personalities start to develop. Other people, by responding to these efforts of ours, help us to measure our progress: How good am I?

It may seem incredibly obvious to a grown-up that trusting another human being can be a great risk. How, though, have you come to this understanding? Like me, you've learned from your own experience, beginning in childhood. We're never more vulnerable than when we trust someone—but, paradoxically, if we cannot trust, neither can we find love or joy.

What does a child learn?

A child learns to trust.

How much confidence we have as we face risks later in our lives—how easily we can separate ourselves from what is familiar to us—is a measure of our maturity. More, the risks of our childhood—how we learn to trust ourselves and others—remain risks we face all our lives:

EVERY CHILD'S THREE QUESTIONS

1. **Can I be myself?**
2. **Can I say what I feel?**
3. **Can I be loved?**

Considering that all of us began as howling and helpless infants completely dependent on other people, it's no wonder that throughout our lives we share a sense of vulnerability, a fear of being separated from—or rejected by—those we depend on or those we think we need.

For years I suffered some of my most miserable moments for fear of being humiliated, for fear that people I thought were "better" would reject me because I wasn't good enough: *What will I do when they find out I'm me?* How about you? Have you ever walked away from a person thinking that you'd really like to know him or her, but you said nothing—for fear that you weren't good enough, for fear that you'd reveal your inadequacy?

But what really happens when someone reveals himself? How do we actually react when a person we've met exposes his anxiety to us, shows us his fears and what he thinks are his weaknesses? Almost always, we feel close to him. We want to help. We want to share our anxieties with him, include him—if only for the moment—in our group. When someone discloses to us his hopes and aspirations, his fears and mistakes, the revelation often challenges our own preconceptions about that person. That's the result we seek when we advise someone to spend more time with a friend: "You'll like him when you get to know him!"

"But if I say too much," the fear haunts us, "the other person will know how stupid I am, how unworthy I am." The vice president will discover I'm not a vice president, the scientist will realize my ignorance of science, the psychologist will perceive my innermost thoughts, the educated person will see my folly—all in twenty minutes of conversation. Or so we think.

Can anyone be known that quickly? How many years, how many thousands of intense hours, has it taken psychiatrists to "know" their patients—sometimes, after all that, only to be wrong. When we're really honest with ourselves, we realize that in our early contacts with another human being only two things may become clear: how similar our attitudes and beliefs are to those of the other person and how that person's needs relate to our own. But that information, however interesting, is small potatoes compared with the truth:

What we really respond to when meeting someone else is the degree of interest the other person shows in us.

Aren't we most complimented when someone asks us about ourselves or asks us for advice? When someone tells us that our opinion matters?

The approach to take when you join small groups or when you meet people for the first time is not to fret about what other people might learn about you but to *focus on what you'd like to learn from them.* This gets anxiety working for you. In other words, it helps you worry well.

It took me many years to recognize that my nervousness when meeting strangers was normal and healthy, that the anxiety I felt could be positive and could help sharpen my questions and underline the sincerity of my interest:

If we remember to spend the first minute or two putting the other fellow at ease, we'll put ourselves at ease too.

To communicate your sincere interest in another person after you've introduced yourself, you might find useful some methods that I've learned and practiced and that have worked for me:

SIX WAYS TO HAVE
A SUCCESSFUL CONVERSATION

1. **Show a real interest.**
    Do more than listen. Nod, smile, or frown when it's appropriate. It's not just the speaker who needs to demonstrate, to be active; a good audience responds. I've been told that I look like one of those plastic dogs with the moving head when I

listen. Once, during a job interview, the executive who was evaluating me talked incessantly. Truly, I did not contribute five words. I later saw his report, in which he described me as "bright." Why? Because I listened to him. Good listeners, like precious gems, are to be treasured. Be an active, enthusiastic listener.

2. **Use the magic word: "Why?"**
   Ask open-ended questions. Do your best to avoid asking questions that are easily answered with a "yes" or "no." Such questions tend to lead to boring conversation, shorten discussion, and can unintentionally sound more like a prisoner's interrogation than a friendly dialogue. "Why?" is a wonderful word with magical qualities to sustain talk. Use it frequently—and learn to love its friends: "Who?" "What?" "When?" "Where?" "How?" They all will improve the conversation—and how!

3. **Say the other person's name.**
   Use the other person's name frequently in the conversation. Each of us responds to the sound of his or her own name. If you repeat a name often, you probably will not forget it; but if you do forget a name at any time, apologize and ask for it again.

4. **Agree heartily; disagree softly.**
   If you must disagree, frame it in a polite question. If that doesn't work, soften your approach: "I'm not sure I feel the same way, but I'm really interested in how you arrived at your conclusion."

Absolutes ("I'm sorry, but I can't agree!") stop a conversation cold.

5. **Let the other person talk.**
   No matter how knowing you are about a subject, the other person is probably more interested in what he or she has to say. And remember that if you're talking, you're not learning. You already know what *you* know.

6. **Don't correct or change the subject.**
   How do you like to be corrected? Or, for that matter, to be interrupted? Do neither. It's also rude to ask someone a question, wait for the answer, then respond by bringing up another topic.

But what do I do if I meet someone who is so mean, angry, or provocative that a healthy conversation simply is not possible?

Excuse yourself and walk away. Sadly, some folks want others to feel their pain, to hurt as much as they do—or more. My grandmother once told me to avoid colds and angry people whenever I could. It's sound advice.

This is a good time to review, from Challenge No. 1 in the first chapter, the examples you've been observing of true hope versus false hope: How did others respond differently to the people who lived with true hope and to the people who lived with false hope? In each example, what did the person involved seem to be focusing on?

You've probably discovered what I and so many of the students of *The Confidence Course* have found: True hope is a far healthier attitude than false hope for the individuals themselves—and others are more at ease with, and respond far more favorably to, people who live with true hope. I suspect you've also noted by now that the people who lived with true hope tended to focus on solutions, while the others did not. This is significant. Anxiety and fear produce energy. Where we focus that energy noticeably affects the quality of our lives:

Focus on the solution, not the problem.

When faced with a disturbing challenge, however large or small, ask yourself: "Am I dwelling on the problem or am I focusing on a solution?" Do not waste worry. If you're going to worry, worry *well.* Put that energy to good use; aim it at an answer. Don't forget: Nothing diminishes anxiety faster than action.

CHALLENGE NO. 5: MAKE SOMEONE ELSE COMFORTABLE

For this next exercise, keep in mind what you've just read about where to focus your energy and review again the following two points:

1. What we really respond to when meeting someone is the degree of interest the other person shows in us.

2. If we remember to spend the first minute or two putting the other fellow at ease, we'll put ourselves at ease too.

Paying particular attention to asking *open-ended questions*, practicing *active listening,* and making frequent use of the *other person's name* will put most people at ease. Do this with at least six different people. Practice the techniques from the first four challenges. Your sole goal in this exercise is to make somebody else comfortable. Earn yourself an A—take advantage of every opportunity you have in the next few days. And, yes, record the results.

5

What I Am, What I Have, What I Seem to Be

Confidence, as I said before, is an attitude—that is, a system of beliefs that predisposes us to see the world in a certain way. It's a filter through which all of our life experiences pass, a filter that we human beings start forming in our brains from our very first stirrings.

Consider fear. For the most part, fear is a filter too. The only fears we're born with, in fact, are the fear of falling and the startle reflex in response to loud noises. We later learn all the rest—and many of those fears are useful and necessary, helping us to survive in dangerous situations. It's certainly wise, for example, to respect fire; on the other hand, it's unwise to be so cautious that you can't cook a hot meal. As Mark Twain observed, a cat that leaps onto a hot stove will not leap onto a hot stove again—but neither will it try a cold one. To enlarge ourselves, to grow in confidence, we need to make a leap that Mark Twain's cat would not make.

You've taken a step in that direction, made an act of trust, by enrolling in *The Confidence Course*. Stay with me. Take another step, one that begins by recognizing a basic law of learning:

Organisms repeat responses that have brought satisfaction in the past, and these responses often persist even when they no longer bring satisfaction.

It's true of a simple protozoan, and it's true of a complex human being. Almost every freshman psychology student reads how the Russian physiologist Ivan Pavlov conditioned his dogs to salivate at the sound of a bell, even when they were no longer rewarded with food.

How about us?

It would be rare for any of us never to have acted childlike at least once while facing some adult challenge—to have never repeated behavior, however inappropriate, that was learned in our earliest years. I know I've pretended at times that something I've really wanted—but was afraid to take a risk for—was not important to me. I'll bet you have too. When we deny what we really desire, we most resemble the small child shouting, "I don't want that toy anyway!"

Inevitably, when we try to avoid making choices or try to escape risk in our lives, when we limit our opportunities to grow, we feel more helpless, more dependent, more vulnerable—in other words, more childlike. Clearly, confidence comes from doing. And to know what we're doing when we consider the crucial challenges of our lives—to muster our courage—we need to understand not only what but *how* we've learned.

Again, *we are what we think*. The world in which we live is shaped by how we see it. To one person, what lies ahead is an empty acre. To another, it's a field to be plowed. For the most part, we are not born as either optimists or pessimists. One of us learns to see danger while another learns to see opportunity. You and I can learn; we can learn to see more clearly.

To start, let's look at how deeply the old, familiar ways are ingrained in our personalities. Do you remember how much of your own childhood involved learning what not to do? *Don't touch this! Don't swallow that! Don't walk there! Leave that alone!* This, while the most profound message of all often went unsaid: *Do what I tell you to do.* Do you remember? Really remember? When we are young, independence rarely brings rewards. Rebellious responses more often inspire guilt or punishment.

Wait a minute! My parents loved me and only wanted the best for me, only wanted to keep me safe!

I have no reason to doubt your parents' love or concern. What I'm urging you to consider is that much of what we remember glows with a halo of virtue: Our elders were bigger, stronger, wiser. As you say, they loved us. All the more reason that what we've learned needs to be examined.

All right, but why?

To gain confidence, we need to have a true picture of who we are and where we belong. For example, I'd like to think of myself as a good and capable and loving parent. Yet, despite boundless love and a background in the social sciences, I've made mighty big mistakes as a father. I've unwittingly transmitted some of my own insecurities to my children, as has my wife. Both of us undoubtedly have sheltered our son and our daughter from too many risks, and too often we've likely emphasized danger over opportunity, vulnerability over strength. Why? Because we love our children dearly, and we worry about their safety and their future. Sometimes our worry overwhelms our good sense: We are parents. The point is not to punish your folks for being as imperfect as my wife and I, but to ask the important questions of yourself that will lead you to learn who you really are, so you can get where you want to go with confidence.

I have such a question, and it troubles me.
Last year,
at thirty-nine years of age, I began a second career.
I feel I'm doing well. Nevertheless,
I seem to constantly
compare myself with friends
who do better financially.
How can I stop these comparisons and
focus on my own abilities?

It's normal to want to measure yourself against other people, even your friends, to see how you're doing. But, as you recognize, how well your friends succeed is a measure of their performance, not yours. Every successful athlete learns that the best way to improve performance is to play against a better player. If, on the other hand, your self-esteem depends solely upon running faster, dressing better, or earning more than someone else, you will be disappointed. There will always be someone who can outdo you, now and in the future. Competition can bolster confidence, however, when the real goal is to improve yourself and not merely to beat someone else.

Did you ever notice that good performers, like athletes, are always raising the bar a little higher? They get better and better because they challenge *themselves*. When you have the right perspective, you can feel tremendous fulfillment. I think you are on track. Your attitude is healthier and more stable than you may realize, because you've acknowledged a profound truth:

The *only* reason to compete is to improve yourself.

Just by the act of asking this difficult question, you already have moved yourself well along the road to changing your focus. I think you'll find what follows—an examination of adolescence, then adulthood—particularly useful.

One day, like an egg bursting from within, the shell of the child falls away. Suddenly, there stands before us a human being who bristles with indignation, a moody stranger who can, at the slightest provocation, be intolerant, rebellious, rude, boastful, even deceitful. We call this season of our lives *adolescence;* for our parents, it's a lot like waltzing with a porcupine.

Only yesterday, it seems, we were looking to adults for approval and support. Now, in our teens, with the eggshell fragments of our childhood falling about us, we erupt. We're not sure whether we're good or bad, powerful or weak—whether we're men or boys, women or girls. Often, with bluster and arrogance, we try to hide the uncertainty we feel inside. Confused, depressed, and often *frightened*, we may act selfish, distrustful, impetuous. On the one hand, life is a joyous discovery, an awakening. On the other, it baffles and flusters us. Pimples mottle our skin; hair sprouts from hidden places; our voices crack; erotic dreams emerge. We crave the ability to understand, to control what's happening to us.

Urgently we ask: "Who am I?"

The question, of course, pops up throughout our lives, but at no time do we seek the answer with more fervor or with more reckless abandon—and never does the answer seem more elusive. *Who am I?*

Children learn when to trust; *adolescents search for identity.*

It's during our teenage years, as we begin our struggle to discover who and what we are, that our lives seem most chaotic. We dive into situations we're not quite ready to handle, inevitably groping our way through one mess after another. Seeking control, we're often out of control. Life is in the extreme. We are either girls or women, boys or men, good or bad, superior or inferior. There are no shades of gray.

We're convinced that no one, particularly our parents, can understand what we're feeling. Thus we try to hide our terrible self-doubt. Uncertainty is denied; we speak with authority—*false* authority. We live in a world of worst and best.

Do you remember, *really* remember?

When we're teenagers, we undergo swift, radical change. Frequently, we act out our confused emotions by renouncing loudly and unequivocally any suggestion that threatens to reveal what we may truly feel—the secret doubts we may have about ourselves. We're stuck on a speeding roller coaster, flailing about as we try to slow it, turn it, direct it, understand it.

Alone, we cry, *"What's happening to me?"*

We're growing up.

We're learning to think for ourselves; we're taking risks. Instinctively, we push away the very people who are closest to us, who've been teaching us, caring for us—so that we may learn to draw our own conclusions. We experiment, with results that are possibly rewarding, possibly comical, possibly tragic.

More, adolescence does not stop like a clock at the end of our teen years, as is commonly believed. For most of us, this stage of our lives continues through our twenties—or, for some, beyond. We've all known adults who try to hide what they really fear by taking risks that are clearly rash, reckless, self-destructive; who take risks for all the wrong reasons; who antagonize, posture, and greedily seek to acquire money or power yet never seem to have enough to feel satisfied; who display love flamboyantly yet never seem to like themselves; and who, whether their risks succeed or fail, never seem to learn from their experiences.

Childish?

No, *adolescent*.

That's why this passage is important. Often, when an adult is told he's acting like a child, he's not being childish at all, but adolescent. We need to know the difference.

Picture three large steps: The first is childhood; next up is adolescence; the highest is our adult years. Now let's look a little more closely at what we've constructed. The first step is actually a series of countless little steps. We grow from our first cell; we become less helpless with each passing day. A newborn is considerably different from a terrible two; a three-year-old is certainly not a nine-year-old. It's easy to marvel at how our bodies evolve. Even more impressive, though, is what happens, unseen, within our brains. Social scientists have discovered that somewhere between the ages of two and four we start to know right from wrong; and later, between roughly eight and ten, we begin to understand the concept of justice.

Adolescence, like childhood, is made up of steps within a step—and this tumultuous stage of our lives generally does not end in our teens or even in our early twenties, as I noted earlier.

I realize it would be foolish or impossible to attempt to assign precise dates at which human lives change. Roughly drawn, though, there are three phases, or tiers, to the approximately twenty-year period we know as adolescence:

THE THREE PHASES OF ADOLESCENCE

Phase One, from about ten or twelve to about seventeen or eighteen.

Our struggle for identity begins in earnest: We ask ourselves, "Who am I?" We're self-absorbed. It's our most volatile time. The triangle is classic: us, our parents, our friends. Emotionally, we try to separate ourselves from our parents while, at the same time, we're drawn irresistibly to our peers for approval. Although we often shout for noncomformity, rarely in our lives are we so conforming. On the one hand, we reject the adult world; but on the other, we adopt language, clothes, and a style so similar to our friends that an observer would think we were all stamped from a giant cookie-cutter. We live for the present, for the moment; we fantasize a future of great success with minimal effort: "I'm going to be rich! I'm going to be famous!"

Phase Two, from about eighteen or nineteen to our early twenties.

The future has become a concern. We're worried; we no longer can shut out the adult world. We ask ourselves: "What am I going to do? I must do something. But what? Who am I?" We test ourselves, often leaving home. Our career plans change, our expectations are sometimes lowered, and our choices start to focus more on self-support. We grow more confident as we successfully face challenges on our own. Because the dramatic changes of puberty are over, we're more comfortable with our bodies than we were earlier.

Phase Three, from our middle to late twenties.
We have a better idea of what our lives will be. We're testing our strengths and limits—but, still self-absorbed, we're not as confident as we appear. We look like adults. We may even be married, have children, appear quite successful—but subtle and substantial adjustments to the adult world continue. As we struggle, inexorably drawn to adulthood, our insecurity flares up and we challenge relationships at home and in the workplace. Again, we ask, "Who am I?"

Rejection is never more terrifying than in adolescence. I'm sure that when I was a teenager I would have been surprised, if not flabbergasted, to be told that one day—*today*—I would write with conviction that vulnerability could make me stronger. I know now, though, that *the approval of someone else is truly satisfying only when I've risked being rejected as I really am.* Every time we're accepted by others after disclosing what we truly feel, one more brick is firmly cemented into the building of our personalities. Only by taking risks, by exposing ourselves to embarrassment, do we grow stronger, tougher, and better able to handle being rejected. Often what we fear most when we're adolescents, ironically, is the very process by which we learn to deal with rejection:

By revealing ourselves, we gain the true confidence that comes only from being accepted as we really are.

But who *are* we?

It is true that we need others to help us explore our identities—but, finally, each of us must answer alone, "Who am I?"

I believe that we can know ourselves in three ways, and how we respond to each of these perceptions helps us to define our personalities.

THREE WAYS WE KNOW OURSELVES

1. **What I am** is who I am when I am alone—my inner self—the whole complex framework of my abilities, both inherited and learned, my choices, my feelings, my fantasies, my desires. It is my essence.

2. **What I have** are my possessions, all that I own. Clothes tear, though. Houses age. Cars rust. Fortunes rise and fall. I think an anecdote once told to me by the Nobel laureate Elie Wiesel illustrates well the fragile nature of what we believe we possess:

> Noting the meager possessions of a wise and famous rabbi—and deeply disappointed by the simple manner in which the rabbi lived despite his worldwide acclaim—a tourist rudely inquired, "Sir, is this all you have?"
>
> The rabbi smiled, pointed to the tourist's suitcase and asked, "Is that all *you* have?"
>
> "Of course," replied the tourist, "but I'm only passing through."
>
> The rabbi nodded.
>
> "So am I," he said.

3. **What I seem to be** is the opinion of me as held by others. How we are seen by someone else, though, is more delicate—and often less sensible—than holding our possessions too tightly. As an editor, for example, how might I be described by the author whose manuscript I accept? And how might I be described by the author whose work I reject? Is one view more accurate than the other? As a father, how am I regarded by my children when I say "yes"? When I say "no"?

Invariably, adolescents seek to find themselves both in their possessions (notice the sudden interest in clothes!) and, with even more intensity, in the approval of their peers. *What I am; what I have; what I seem to be:* Which of these three we're most eager to take a risk for—what is most important to us—is a sure gauge of our maturity and a sign of our self-confidence.

Okay, I agree. I know myself only when I weigh "what I am" over those other concerns. I understand what you've said about trust being the most important thing I learned as a child. And I recognize how utterly absorbed I've been as an adolescent. But what makes an adult?

Children learn when to trust; adolescents search for identity; *adults see beyond themselves.*

Picture yourself in front of a mirror fogged with steam.

Wipe away the moisture. Do you see yourself? Now imagine that you were able to rub that mirror so hard that the silver backing disappeared and the glass became a window. *When we can see past our own reflection—when we see and care beyond ourselves, when we see and learn from others— only then do we become adults.* As a child learning to trust, we begin to wipe away the moisture from the mirror. As an adolescent in search of an identity, we stare at the reflection. As an adult, it is our acceptance of who we are, blemishes and all, that allows us to wipe away the silver. The world is a hard and unpredictable arena. Only when we learn to say with conviction, "I accept who I am," are we adequately prepared to look beyond ourselves, to face risk—and loss— as an adult.

Now, this may surprise—and relieve—you: All of the most successful human beings I have known were inwardly at war with themselves. Their turmoil was at least as great as our own, and sometimes greater. What distinguished these leaders was not some inner peace but rather how they had learned to organize their lives around a noble ambition and to focus on it: *Children learn when to trust; adolescents search for identity; adults see beyond themselves.*

Many people have told me over the years that they want to be happy. Yet I know that's not what they want. If I say something funny and make them laugh, that's *happy*. It's not "happy" they seek; they seek to be *fulfilled*.

I believe the challenges worth taking are those that lead to the most fulfilling life. When we commit to high ideals, we succeed before the outcome is known. This is the basis of the second of the Seven Steps to Self-Fulfillment:

THE SECOND STEP TO SELF-FULFILLMENT

1. Know who is responsible.
   Accept personal responsibility for your behavior. When you say, "I am responsible," you can build a new life, even a new world.
2. **Believe in something big.**
   Your life is worth a noble motive.

Now here's the thing: It's not possible for either you or me to be an empty bucket. Human beings are not made that way. You carry in your skull a computer more sophisticated and more powerful than all the devices created by the engineers of IBM, Apple, Compaq, and Microsoft combined. As long as you live, your brain cannot be barren or vacant. Something is always going on up there.

How many functions do you think your brain is performing right now? It's processing the symbols of your language and using the alphabet it has memorized while it monitors your temperature and the environment, measures digestion, guides the conversion of fuel to energy, simultaneously directs and moves body parts . . . on and on, all in microseconds! Your brain accomplishes so many tasks simultaneously, at the speed of light, that its sheer power is breathtaking, its memory capacity so vast that it can't be accurately measured.

This magnificent piece of hardware has been engineered to run efficiently full to the brim—but, sadly, too often we've been conditioned to believe just the opposite. Some folks, for example, are convinced that they can be empty, that they can believe in nothing. Those folks are wrong, of course.

Sometimes *we* are "those folks." From childhood on, we have been encouraged to respect limits and often have been told what not to do. It's not surprising, under the circumstances, to find us believing that we are not defined by our own choices, but that life happens *to* us and is not determined *by* us. When I say, "Believe in something big," a little voice inside me may be quick to respond, "I am too small." Our instruction (what social scientists call "socialization") is frequently subtle—powerfully subtle. We learn to honor heroes, for example, which in itself is okay. At the same time, unfortunately, we've been encouraged to make these heroes distinct from us—as if we could not walk side by side with them.

Joan of Arc, Abraham Lincoln, Mohandas Gandhi, Winston Churchill, Eleanor Roosevelt, Clara Barton, Frederick Douglass, Marie Curie, Martin Luther King Jr., Harry Truman . . . do they seem, well, larger than life? Yet what were they? Human beings, with brains and bodily functions. I do not seek to disparage or diminish their contributions. On the contrary, the fact that they were human beings, not gods, and achieved so much gives you and me true hope. These people are examples, models. The shame is that we've been invited since childhood to be fans rather than teammates when, in this game of life, we're players too. You can shout, "Hey, Coach, play me!" and be heard.

We create ourselves, as I've said, by the choices we make, and thus we choose who we want to be. Again, we are what we *think*. And we are never empty. No person who has ever lived has been an unbeliever, despite what he or she may argue. Every one of us believes *something*. Maybe we have faith in God—or in no God. Maybe it's money or power or a career or a position, a friend, a spouse, parents. Perhaps we look to science. Some of us may choose to think that nothing matters—which is particularly sad, because what we believe, whatever we place before ourselves, is what we run toward. Other people might embrace a mission, a goal, a principle—*something*.

What do you believe? Even more important, what do you believe *in*? It should be yourself. Let me help you.

It would be foolish to suggest that I could discuss enough in this chapter—or in this course—to thoroughly examine the depth and breadth of a human life. I know that the stages of our lives cannot be mapped with pinpoint accuracy: Life is sloppy; seasons overlap. What I've sought to do here, by tracing how we grow, is to encourage you to reflect, to candidly and aggressively search your background for the hidden obstacles that can hold you back.

When we cling like a child to some false notion, however secure it makes us feel, we not only retard our personal growth but also make it far more difficult—and danger-ous—to take the risks we need to build confidence. To learn to be more confident, whether we feel frightened or only vaguely uneasy when we face a difficult challenge, it's criti-cal to be honest, to ask: "What am I responding to? Whom am I trying to please?"

Children learn when to trust; adolescents search for iden-tity; adults see beyond themselves: To be an adult, you must wrap yourself around something larger than you—because *your life is worth a noble motive.* This not only underlies your efforts but also gives meaning to them. Remember, we human beings share a universal experience that can be described in a word, a word that applies to the child born two thousand years ago or the child yet to be conceived. It is true of every culture, of every tribe that has ever existed or will ever exist—of all people, all races, all languages. The word is *struggle.* We all do it. And we all survive, we all endure until that last heartbeat. A rare and precious few seem to do more. They prevail—and it's in their lives that we may find meaning for our own.

CHALLENGE NO. 6: JOIN A TEAM

List the people, living or dead, whom you admire because of how they've led their lives. In other words, *whose team would you like to join?*

Do this assignment slowly. It may take a while, and

that's fine. Research the subject as thoroughly as if you were writing a term paper. Instead of a long dissertation, however, write down *the best single word or sentence that describes the meaning of that person's mission*. Before you start, give it some thought. Then you'll be ready. And please don't make this heavy. Even Nobel laureates like Elie Wiesel and Mairead Corrigan Maguire have a sense of humor, despite the horrors they've seen in the Nazi concentration camps or Northern Ireland. There's no gray cloud of gloom hanging over their heads.

You're looking for a principle to practice.

Keep in mind that this assignment is not meant to encourage you to shed your loved ones, cast off all of your possessions, and head to the mountaintop in search of a great thought. What I'd like you to do is to *touch the world around you*. If the word you discover is "kindness," for example, embrace the principle and be kind to those whom you encounter every day in and out of your home and your neighborhood.

Keep your mission specific:

I remember a teenage girl I met years ago in a commune. I was a newspaper reporter conducting interviews for a feature article. The girl volunteered to me the meaning of life, as she saw it:

"Love," she said.

"What do you mean?" I inquired.

"I love mankind!" she told me.

"How about him?" I asked, pointing to a young man

seated nearby whose personal hygiene was suspect.

She paused and slowly shook her head "no," then repeated: "I love mankind!"

Sometimes, as with my teenage friend, it's easier to embrace what we don't have to touch. As I said, you're looking for *a principle to practice*. I know you'll find it.

6

How to Overcome Shyness

Some say shyness is in the genes. Others argue that we learn to be shy. Who knows? Maybe someday we'll find out. In the meantime, if you suffer bouts of shyness as I do, you may find what I've learned to be useful, solid advice that can help you act confidently when you are most ill at ease.

First, though, you need to recognize that our shyness does not define us. When we are shy, we tend to see shyness as the largest part of our personality. That's simply wrong. Being shy is only a tiny piece of who we are, and our shyness is far less important to others than it is to us.

That understood, here are six practical steps you can take to overcome shyness:

SIX STEPS TO OVERCOMING SHYNESS

1. **Find common ground.**
   Crowds can be overwhelming. If you have to join a large crowd, you will be less nervous if you are there with a friend or two. I can be comfortable in the largest of groups if I am there with a few people I know.

2. **Plan ahead.**
   Before you leave home, decide what you are going to say. You don't need to prepare a "state of the union" address or memorize a comedy routine. Simply ask questions—the technique you learned in Chapter 4: How to Start a Conversation.

3. **Move your body.**
   It may sound funny, but this really helps. Physical activity—action—dispels nervous energy. (This does not mean that you should propel your body as fast as possible to the door.)

4. **Stop looking at yourself.**
   Focus on others. Shy people focus on themselves, on their fears and anxieties of the moment. Keep in mind that all of us respond to the degree of interest another person shows in us. So, if we remember to spend the first minute or two putting the other fellow at ease, we'll put ourselves at ease too.

5. **Find a prop.**
   They're useful for starting conversations: "That's an unusual ring. How was it designed?" (You might sometimes carry a prop yourself, which makes it a little

easier for others to engage you—particularly if they
have read this passage.) At other times, circumstances
can be your ticket to talk. If you are at a tennis
tournament, for example, you can discuss tennis.
Romances and friendships tend to be built at school
and in the workplace because people there have
something in common to talk about. So, take
advantage: Almost all initial conversations are a search
for a common interest.

6. **Smile.**
Have you ever noticed how easily puppies make human
friends? Yet all they do is wag their tails and fall over. If
you give yourself a friendly attitude, others will notice.

7

How to Handle Mistakes:
"SLIP" and "RIP"

A few days before I was to perform a one-person show at Ford's Theatre in Washington, D.C., a colleague of mine at *Parade* magazine asked why I would open in a place where so many people would see me.

"If I were you," he advised, "I'd find the smallest theater I could in northern Connecticut to open the show, and I'd make sure only a dozen seats were filled."

"Yes, you would," I agreed.

"I don't understand," he said. "You're an editor and a writer, not an actor. You don't have to do this. Why are you opening there, in front of people from the White House, celebrities, so many people who know you, even other performers?"

"I've thought a lot about that," I admitted, "and I know why I want to do it this way. You see, I can fail just as easily in a small, empty theater in northern Connecticut as I can in Ford's Theatre with the seats filled. But I didn't work this hard—hundreds of hours of writing and rehearsing—to have a little flop. If I'm going to fail, I want to fail big."

The first six chapters examined who you are and what's important to you. In this chapter we'll explore why it's not only healthy but even necessary for all of us to make mistakes. In the following chapter, we'll also begin to take a close look at one of the oldest and most entertaining ways we have to relate to one another—storytelling.

First, though, I'd like to review Challenge No. 3. I'm sure that by now you've found from your daily diary that most of what we worry about never happens. I first gave this assignment more than two decades ago to a class I was teaching in abnormal psychology at Westchester Community College in Valhalla, New York. To this day, wherever and whenever I've suggested this exercise, the results have been similar:

Most worries just don't happen. Much of what we worry about happens for the good, not the bad, and only the tiniest fraction of what we fear actually occurs. I suspect you've already learned by this time that you eliminate a large number of worries simply by writing them down. It's also probably apparent at this point that many worries are vague or silly. It's true for everybody. Another important insight for nearly every student has been that when we try to measure the possible consequences of what we're concerned about—when we ask ourselves, "What's the worst thing that can happen?"—very often our anxieties diminish because we discover in so many cases that the worst isn't that bad after all.

I realize that you probably have not completed the thirty days of diary-keeping, and yet you may feel that you've learned enough from this exercise. Still, I'd like you to continue writing your journal. And, again, please do not share the results until you've experienced the full month. Then, if you'd like to discuss it with someone else—go ahead. A note of caution, however: This exercise works so well because it lets you discover for yourself the truth about your worries. If you want to assist others, be sure to allow them to experience the impact of this discovery on their own. If you reveal too early what you now know, the power of the exercise will be diminished. When you let other people live this exercise as you have, the effect on their worries will be very similar to what you've seen happen to yours.

We change constantly. Just as our cells die and are replenished every few months, new ideas present themselves continuously, opportunities bubble forth—and our magnificent brains, all the while, keep processing millions of bits of information every day. If we're going to recognize and take advantage of the openings life affords us and at the same time worry well, we must accept this fundamental rule:

To succeed, we must be prepared to fail.

Life, after all, is trial and error. One of the greatest Olympic divers of the twentieth century, Greg Louganis, once told me that a million fans may witness a dive that the judges score a perfect ten, but none sees the thousand imperfect dives that preceded it in practice, the thousand it actually took to create that single ten.

Sherry Lansing, who was the first woman in the history of Hollywood to run a major movie studio and who is now one of America's most accomplished producers, observed: "I have seen really good people make really big mistakes, but they're the same people who create giant successes."

True success is always the last of a string of failed attempts to get it right.

If we did not test, did not experiment, did not try, did not flub, we would not grow.

Look outside. Nature has been correcting itself, successfully adapting to new circumstances, since the first cell split and didn't look quite like the original. A rattlesnake is not a cobra, and neither is a worm. Have you ever seen two identical maple trees? Is a crocodile a chameleon? Is a rat a hamster? If our cave-dwelling ancestors had not tried—and failed—so many times, you and I, if we existed at all, might be throwing stones at the moon tonight to chase away the clouds. Not only would life be unproductive without error, it also would be boring. The opportunity to learn would be lost. It's not whether we make mistakes that matters, it's understanding the opportunity they afford us.

I'm confused. You seem to be defining "mistakes"
differently from what I have learned.
What, exactly, is a mistake?

A mistake can be several different things. It can be a wrong choice or a misunderstanding, which probably is how you've come to understand the word. But a mistake also can be a decision whose results simply are different from what we expected. It can be, as Greg Louganis indicated, a practice dive or a rehearsal to achieve a better performance. I have rewritten this paragraph, for example, five times. It has shrunk from more than a hundred words to fewer than eighty. (Oops, fewer than ninety.)

From my own experience, I've learned to recognize at least four kinds of mistakes other than those necessary to improve performance. I remember them by using the acronym SLIP, short for mistakes of similarity, lapse, ignorance, and perception:

THE FOUR SLIPS: SIMILARITY, LAPSE, IGNORANCE, PERCEPTION

1. **Mistakes of Similarity**
   These probably account for the majority of our errors. We often repeat behavior when signals seem similar. We might rise one Monday morning, dress for work, hoist a briefcase, open a car door, sit behind a familiar steering wheel, and drive to the place where we used to work rather than to where we work now. A stranger reminds us of someone we know, and we respond as if the stranger were that familiar person. Or we complete an important report and toss it in the wastepaper basket as if it were trash. Familiarity prompts these mistakes, but it is important to recognize that the same behavior could

easily have been correct. We erred because we responded to familiar signals that existed under different conditions.

2. **Mistakes of Lapse**
   Our memory takes a hike. You plan a route to complete some errands and forget several anyway. You're interrupted by a telephone call as you clean your room, and you leave the house after the call without finishing the room. You can't recall where you've put your coat. You walk into the kitchen and can't remember why you entered the room. Or, more seriously, you forget to take your medicine, have the brakes checked, or complete an important assignment for work or school.

3. **Mistakes of Ignorance**
   We *know* we don't know, but we act anyway. These mistakes run from the humorous (ordering from a foreign menu and finding something unfamiliar staring back at you from the plate) to something that can have tragic consequences ("What is there to handling a boat?").

4. **Mistakes of Perception**
   We *think* we know. We mistakenly assume on a chilly day that the water in a swimming pool has been heated, so we plunge in. Often we insist on making these mistakes. When we vehemently argue a point based on information that we're not sure exists, only to discover later that the information indeed does not exist, we commit a mistake of perception. Our desire overwhelms reality, and we blunder because we refuse to see.

Now, there is a fifth mistake, which would be to think that I have covered everything in those four. No doubt we could squeeze errors into more types, but SLIP covers a large number that we can agree on. Whether your mistake is a step to improve performance or a SLIP, remember:

When you do nothing, you don't make mistakes; when you don't make mistakes, you do nothing.

Are you saying you want me to make mistakes?

Absolutely. I want you to make mistakes—because I wish for you the most joyous life possible. There's no real joy in emptiness, in doing nothing, in risk-free living: *True success is always the last of a string of failed attempts to get it right.* In order to live a fulfilled life, to feel exhilarated by your accomplishments, to worry well, you must expect mistakes to occur—and you must practice what I call RIP, a second acronym, which stands for responsibility, insight, and perspective. It also means, as you know, "rest in peace," which in itself may not be a bad way to look at your mistakes.

RIP MISTAKES: RESPONSIBILITY, INSIGHT, PERSPECTIVE

1. **Responsibility**

   Accept responsibility for your errors; you will find no better time to practice the first of the Seven Steps to Self-Fulfillment: *I am responsible.* A mistake does not mean you're a bad person, it means only that you're one of us, a human being. If failure meant incompetence, we'd still be sleeping in caves. Never ignore mistakes—if you do, you condemn yourself to repeat them. If you own up to a blunder, you can learn from it, which is the next step.

2. **Insight**

You are not your mistake. Study your error only for what you can gain from it. Do not waste time and effort agonizing over your guilt. Ask, "What went wrong? Why? What have I learned so that I can do better next time?" It's a lot easier to be honest with yourself when you recognize that you and your mistake are not the same thing, that you are not a failure because something you do fails.

3. **Perspective**

The vast majority of mistakes are merely problems we have the opportunity to solve. They are rarely personal tragedies. Try not to confuse the possible consequences of a mistake with the mistake itself. To keep perspective—as you've already learned from keeping your personal diary—simply ask yourself, "What's the worst thing that can happen?" The answer will often diminish your fear, because the worst may not be that bad. And even in the rare case when it is that bad, once you've accepted the worst that can happen, you can *focus on the solution, not the mistake,* and let your anxiety work *for* you. Don't resist its force. Instead, use the precious energy that anxiety provides to keep you alert as you explore your possibilities. You've never been sharper.

When you accept responsibility, examine your experience, and focus on solutions, not only do you apply the principles of Responsibility-Insight-Perspective successfully and thus profit from your errors, but you also make your anxiety an ally. RIP isn't just for mistakes; it's for life.

CHALLENGE NO. 7: FOCUS ON SOLUTIONS

Write down on several pieces of paper these three words: *Focus on solutions.* Place these messages where they will get in your way—a pocket, a purse, next to your toothbrush, in your shoes—wherever you'll be sure to see or touch one of them. This is no trick or game; it's a highly effective learning technique.

Over the next few days you'll have contacts, experiences, concerns—situations will arise that require your attention. The messages are purposely placed to disrupt your daily flow, like boulders in a stream. The more messages you plant, the better; this exercise works best when it's annoying. The irritating interruptions will help you to fuse the message—*focus on solutions*—with your actual experiences throughout the day, not just when it's convenient for you to think about it or when you're reading these pages, as you are right now.

Do this exercise for three days. Each time a message pops up, steel yourself to consider once again its meaning and see if there's a situation at hand or one that occurred recently to which you can apply the principles you're studying. Keep in mind that I've described SLIP in this chapter only to assist you to view more broadly the sort of flubs we make every day and to encourage you not to put all your errors under a big blanket called "mistakes." I hope it has helped. It's not necessary to remember the details of SLIP, but it is important to embrace the basic principles of responsibility, insight, and perspective—because that's where the action is.

Now here's another notion you may find useful over the next three days: A sensible way to view errors, especially if you're in a position to evaluate the performance of others, is to recognize that there is a big difference between a mistake of sloth and a mistake of ambition. A mistake of sloth, or laziness, should be discouraged; *a mistake of ambition should be encouraged*.

A mistake of sloth is what occurs when a windshield on an assembly line is not examined because the person responsible is daydreaming about his next fishing trip and just lets the glass go by. It's easy to see that such a mistake must be discouraged.

On the other hand, when an error occurs because an employee is working so hard that something slips by— she's doing the work of two people, for example, filling in for an employee who is out sick—a wise foreman may note the error, but he'll enthusiastically praise and celebrate the effort behind it. Thus, he encourages ambition, hard work, and growth.

During the next seventy-two hours, as you complete this exercise, keep your eyes open for mistakes of ambition versus those of sloth. Pay attention to how these two kinds of mistakes are handled by others: Were the mistakes handled well? If so, why? If not, why not? What would you do differently? Remember, whether we call an error a SLIP or we identify it as ambition or sloth, mistakes are an opportunity to learn and to grow.

Imagine a boy who struggles to earn a B in fifth grade—and he's punished by his father for not receiving a B+ or an A. Working even harder, in the next marking period he earns a B+—and again he's scolded, because it's not an A or an A+. At baseball he leads the team, hitting .350—but Dad reminds him that .350 is not .400.

Hasn't each of us known an individual like this child who, now that he has become an adult, vehemently complains about his current employer or some other authority figure? Having resigned or been fired from a half-dozen jobs, he's able to graphically recount the failings and mistakes of all of his superiors, never recognizing that he's ascribing the same characteristics to different people. More, the supervisors' prime flaws, as he describes them, never seem to vary: "They just don't recognize how valuable I am. I'm not appreciated." Still in pain, still futilely seeking approval, the man jousts with the ghosts of his childhood. He doesn't say, "I hate Dad." That's far too painful to admit. He says instead, "I hate the boss"—transferring his hate to whoever is in authority. The man's hate, though hidden, is complete and real; it is the color of his world.

When someone repeatedly involves us in unpleasant experiences—particularly those that cause us to feel fear, anger, or pain—not surprisingly, we may form an attitude of hate, even if we must suppress it to survive the moment. Blindly seeking release, such concealed, festering hate causes immense pain to countless individuals and is the cause, I suspect, of at least some of the intolerance in the world today.

I've used just one example of intolerance (I'm sure you can imagine many examples that are even more extreme) to introduce the third of the Seven Steps to Self-Fulfillment:

THE THIRD STEP TO SELF-FULFILLMENT

1. Know who is responsible.

    Accept personal responsibility for your behavior. When you say, "I am responsible," you can build a new life, even a new world.

2. Believe in something big.

    Your life is worth a noble motive.

3. **Practice tolerance.**

    You will like yourself a lot more, and so will others.

To explore the value of tolerance, it might be useful to recall here the parable about the two Buddhist monks who were hurrying late one afternoon to return to their monastery before nightfall. Unexpectedly, they came upon a beautiful young woman stranded at the edge of the same river they had to ford. The woman, they observed, was perplexed, pacing, frantic. Like the monks, she was acutely aware that night was approaching.

"The water is so high!" she exclaimed. "How can I possibly get across?"

The taller monk promptly hoisted the young lady onto his back and strode across the swollen river, gently depositing her safely on the other side.

"Thank you so much," she said. Now secure, she walked quickly to the road that would take her home.

The monks started quietly along an adjoining path, but as soon as the young woman was out of sight, the shorter monk launched into an angry litany:

"Have you forgotten your vows? How dare you touch a woman! What will people say? You have scandalized our order, carried our very religion into disrepute. . . . "

The taller monk, his head bowed, walked silently, listening without argument to the dreary, seemingly endless sermon.

Finally, after an hour of monotonous abuse, the taller monk interrupted, "Excuse me, my brother. I dropped that woman by the river. Are you still carrying her?"

Are *you* carrying a heavy load?

I know intimately how ponderous such a burden can

be. In my own life I have hated. I also have felt jealousy, resentment, and prejudice, and I have been intolerant toward others. I know now that none of these ugly feelings ever gave me comfort, helped solve a problem, or made me feel good about myself. When we study mistakes, as we have in this chapter, we learn that they show how human we are, how *different* we are.

Be tolerant: You will like yourself a lot more, and so will others.

8

How to Tell a Story

I am a storyteller. Yet, until now, I've never discussed how I first found out just how important telling stories is to me.

It all began in the fall of 1980, when I was seated in the den of Irving Wallace's home in Brentwood, California. Irving had written more than thirty-five popular novels and nonfiction books—including mammoth best-sellers like *The Chapman Report, The Prize, The Plot, The Man,* and *The Word*—and he was coauthor with his two children of *The Book of Lists* and *The People's Almanac.*

I was there to suggest that Irving, his daughter, Amy, and his son, David, write a column of unusual facts for *Parade,* of which I had only recently become editor. I was very enthusiastic, and I did my best to be persuasive.

Yet, although Irving was cordial and warm, he was non-committal.

Finally I said, "You have almost everything a writer could want in his life."

I had his attention. He was, after all, one of the most prosperous novelists ever.

"Almost?" he asked.

"Yes," I said, "you're just missing one thing."

"What's that?"

In for a penny, in for a pound, I thought. *I hope he has a sense of humor.*

"You're missing me," I replied, "as your editor."

He laughed loudly, and so did I. I'm sure it was then, in that delightful moment—when this enormously successful author was so gracious and good-humored with a very vulnerable young editor—that I knew I had made a friend.

Shortly before Christmas of that same year, Irving called to say that he and his children would do the column I had proposed. "We'll try it for a year," he promised, "and we'll call it *Significa.*"

"Wonderful," I told him.

The column continued not for one but for three years, and it eventually was published as a book—and Irving, his wife, Sylvia, and David and Amy became my friends for life. I've never felt more honored than when I was asked by his family to speak at a memorial service for Irving after he died in 1990.

On the plane ride back to New York after the service, I remembered our first meeting in Irving's home, and I kept weighing the brief exchange of words that has affected me to this day. Irving had been talking about writing, about what he felt was important:

"Walter," he said, "I believe I can tell a story as well as anyone. I am a storyteller."

"So am I!" I replied.

Instantly, two interesting things happened: One, for the first time in my life, I realized that I was a storyteller—that what I had exclaimed was true. And, second, I was completely, utterly embarrassed. My face burned bright red. Incredibly, I had just told one of the planet's great storytellers that, well, I was like him. What could have been a sour moment was instead made glorious because Irving's response was immediate and genuine.

"Yes, you are," he told me.

We discussed storytelling at length, and—as this generous man did for so many others—he encouraged me to write, to tell tales, to discover, to create.

Now, here we are today, you and I, and I have a message, an assurance, that I can say to you with unqualified conviction:

You are a storyteller.

You are. You have been hearing and telling stories all of your life. Like the air we breathe, storytelling is so much a part of our existence that sometimes we take it for granted and fail to recognize its power over us and everyone else. Truly, a well-told story can amuse, disarm, teach, and motivate; it can make a point, win a friend, or close a sale. In this and succeeding chapters, I'm going to take some of the mystery out of the art of storytelling by revealing to you practical techniques to build and tell your stories more effectively.

Since long before recorded history, even before our cave-dwelling ancestors scratched pictographs on cavern walls, storytelling has ignited the imaginations of listeners of every age in every corner of the globe. Generation after generation, in place after place, human beings have told stories to entertain, to instill values, to pass on traditions, to express their hopes and their fears. It is in the stories of the peoples of the earth that we find their history, their dreams, their nightmares.

A standard dictionary description of "story" might say something like, "A story is a narrative, either true or fictitious, in prose or verse, designed to interest, amuse, or instruct the hearer or reader." My, how interesting. Small wonder that so many of us fail to recognize that we are all storytellers. Doesn't that definition read like one of those rules you had to memorize in the fourth grade? You may find a definition that is more user-friendly, but I wouldn't be surprised if you didn't. Many dictionaries have two definitions for "storyteller": The first is "a person who narrates stories," and the second is "a fibber or liar." Since I'm a confessed storyteller, obviously I'm not too keen on the latter definition.

What makes a story interesting? *Tension* and *discovery*. Tension and discovery are what rivet an audience, hold its attention, make a story absorbing. Tension occurs in real life because none of us knows for sure what's going to happen next. Isn't that what makes life interesting? We're curious; we anticipate. The drama unfolds tomorrow. Tension in life is authentic, isn't it? A well-told story is similar—except that the tension of a story is artificially created. Storytellers build tension by asking or implying a question as early in a tale as possible. Whenever that question is answered—when the discovery is made—the tension ends.

When I asked the late Alex Haley—the coauthor of *The Autobiography of Malcolm X* and the author of *Roots*—how to tell a story, he said, "Start at the beginning and tell the earliest thing that happened." I remember one afternoon in San Antonio, Texas, when I listened intently as Alex mesmerized a thousand people in an auditorium—holding all, including me, on the edge of our seats for twenty minutes. His story? He told a tale from his childhood, about a man who walked to church one Sunday in Henning, Tennessee, sat in a pew, and caught a fly in his hand. That's the entire structure of Alex's story—its beginning, middle, and end. True, he filled the story with wonderful details and color, but its power was in its simplicity and, of course, its *tension*.

Alex began his story by describing how several little children in the town followed the man, who was tipsy, as he made his way to church. They were impatient: "Would he be able to do it? Would they see it happen again?" The man ignored their questions, and he stumbled often. The story concluded with the man doing "it"—which was catching a fly in his bare hand, to the oohs and ahhs of the congregation.

As you read the following One-Minute Stories, pay particular attention to how you think tension is created and when discovery occurs. Although these stories are brief, you may still find that sometimes one question leads to another. Yes, the plot thickens. Enjoy.

A CHILD OPENS THE DOOR

You may remember how Robert and Ted Kennedy and the rest of their family kept to themselves in those first few weeks after the assassination of President John F. Kennedy on November 22, 1963.

But no door closes forever.

Robert Kennedy had promised to visit an orphanage during its Christmas party, and he decided to keep his word—thus becoming the first family member to make a public appearance after the death of his older brother.

The distinguished author Peter Maas was there that day, and he told me what happened:

The children rushed forward to greet Senator Kennedy, but—as often happens when we confront celebrities—the group stopped short. In that instant, one little boy blurted out, "Your brother is dead!"

The room went silent. The adults, including Peter, froze.

The little boy—not knowing what he had done wrong—began to cry.

As quickly as he could, the senator crossed the room, scooped the child up in his arms, hugged him, and said softly, "That's all right. I have another."

JUST ONE MORE STEP

When you think it's tough to go on, you might want to remember this story:

At ten minutes to seven on a dark, cool evening in Mexico City in 1968, John Stephen Akwari of Tanzania painfully hobbled into the Olympic Stadium—the last man to finish the marathon.

The winner already had been crowned, and the victory ceremony was long finished. So the stadium was almost empty as Akwari—alone, his leg bloody and bandaged—struggled to circle the track to the finish line. The respected documentary filmmaker Bud Greenspan watched from a distance. Then, intrigued, Bud walked over to Akwari and asked why he had continued the grueling struggle to the finish line.

The young man from Tanzania answered softly: "My country did not send me nine thousand miles to start the race. They sent me nine thousand miles to finish the race."

WHEN THE OTHER PERSON IS RIGHT

Barbara Walters and her producer, Beth Polson, stood apart like two prizefighters.

Beth wanted Barbara to promote an upcoming special with an appearance on Johnny Carson's show. The idea made Barbara nervous. "I'm an interviewer," she said adamantly, "not an interviewee."

Beth persisted. Beth *in*sisted.

Finally Barbara blurted at her friend, "You're a steamroller, and you push me into everything. I don't want to do the Johnny Carson show. Stop steamrolling me!"

Barbara left the office, a knot tightening in her stomach as she walked. She returned, though, and hugged Beth.

She did appear on Johnny's show—and, a year later, she received a small pillow on which was embroidered this question: "Have you hugged your steamroller today?"

Barbara subsequently confessed, "Sometimes the only thing left to do after an outburst is to admit you're wrong and say what you feel. The other person probably hurts too. It's hard to find a way back sometimes, but I think it's important that we try."

CHALLENGE NO. 8:
STORIES ASK QUESTIONS

The three stories I asked you to read are as plain in their construction as was Alex Haley's fly-catcher tale. I'm sure you noticed that there are very few words in each of the One-Minute Stories, yet didn't you want to find out what happened next? On a separate sheet of paper, write down a question that you feel created tension in each of the three stories. Do not spend more than a minute or two on this. When you have the three questions written, put the paper away for now.

The very best stories touch everyone. They pass like an invisible thread through each of us.

Why?

Because *stories contain basic truths of life*. We can identify with them. They mean something to us. Indeed, the
greatest stories transcend time and place. Here's a cen-
turies-old example:

THE FINISH LINE

Have you heard of Diogenes? He was the ancient Greek
philosopher who went about Athens carrying a lantern in
broad daylight, trying to find an honest man.

Diogenes truly was an unconventional thinker, a man
who believed that people held the key to happiness within
themselves and that the simplest life was the healthiest.

During his old age, he made it a point to keep himself
as active as ever. When one of his disciples urged him to
slow down, Diogenes replied, "I know that many people
feel that old age is a time to take it easy, but I compare my
life now to being the last runner in a relay race. Would you
have me slow down as I near the finish line?"

And so the remarkable Diogenes lived until well into his
nineties.

And to those who will listen, he has left his baton.

Can you imagine how many times through the centuries the story of Diogenes has been told to teach or to
inspire? Didn't it cause you to pause and consider, if only
for an instant? Did you ask yourself, "How am I approaching *my* finish line?"

Just about now in every class of *The Confidence Course*, a flurry of hands rise, all signaling a single question:

But where do I find good stories like these to tell?

Stories are everywhere. Let's take a look.

First, you may find the deepest well in your own backyard—*your life experience*. These stories can be among the most interesting. Children love to hear their parents and grandparents talk about themselves as children. Adults, on the other hand, often take for granted how much they too love to hear a good story. They forget how frequently, every day, they themselves casually request a story: When we ask a personal question of someone else, aren't we really asking that person to tell us a story? So, *search your past for incidents that were joyful, silly, or painful.*

This is a good time to examine why you feel the way you do about topics that are important to you. Take this a step further: When did you first realize you felt so strongly about this subject? There's a story there. *Stories are everywhere*. Remember the story I shared with you about the day I found blood on my cheek from a pay telephone—how, in my anger, I swore: "I'm getting out of here"? And when did I first realize I was a storyteller? Yes, the story I told about Irving Wallace.

When we're hunting for stories, each of us has to be careful we're not like the little fish who asks the big fish to help him find the ocean: The big fish says, "This is the ocean. You're swimming in it." But the little fish argues,

"No, I'm told the ocean is vast. This is only water. I want to find the *ocean*!" Stories are around us, near us, in us—so close, it's easy to overlook them. You, my friend, are not only a storyteller, *you are a story*.

Another rich resource is your family history. Talk to your parents, grandparents, or other older members of your family. Get their stories. Pass on your heritage. All families have stories—and the richer a family is in its stories, the greater the legacy it has to pass along.

You'll find that newspaper, radio, and television reports are filled every day with stories. Visit your local library. You'll be genuinely moved by how eager your librarian will be to help you find collections of folk and fairy tales, humorous, scary, and inspiring stories.

Whenever you read or hear that a storyteller is in town, make it a point to attend the performance. (And if I happen to be the storyteller, double the effort and applaud loudly!)

Look around. *Stories are everywhere*. Read an old gravestone, then let your imagination go to work. Visit a historic site or stand in an old house. Let your imagination go to work. Look into the face of a stranger. Note the clothes. Are there clues to a story? I'll bet there are. And, again, let your imagination go to work.

Trust the magic power of imagination. Storytelling fires the imagination like nothing else. Movies and television, even plays, almost always deny us the chance to participate, to imagine. Storytelling, on the other hand, involves us. If, for example, the storyteller says the enchanted princess is beautiful, then you imagine *beautiful* as only you see it—

whatever the word "beautiful" means to you. If you're told the villain is grotesque, you imagine *grotesque* differently from the fellow seated next to you. That's what makes storytelling so special. Everybody hears a story differently—flavored, colored by his or her unique and individual experiences. Movies can be shown to empty houses. Televisions can blare in vacant rooms. (In fact, the darn things often do.) But storytelling needs an audience. Just as the storyteller and the story are inseparable, the audience and the story are inseparable. It makes a difference how a story is told; it makes a difference how a story is heard.

CHALLENGE NO. 9: ALL QUESTIONS ARE GOOD QUESTIONS

Now's the time to retrieve that sheet of paper from Challenge No. 8, on which you wrote the question that you feel created tension in each of the One-Minute Stories I asked you to read. Compare what you perceived in these stories with the following, which are actual responses from the first three people to whom I gave the same instruction:

A CHILD OPENS THE DOOR

Reader 1: What did Robert Kennedy do?
Reader 2: What's going to happen when Robert Kennedy makes his first appearance after his brother's assassination?

100

Reader 3: What happens when a vulnerable person makes a hurtful mistake?

JUST ONE MORE STEP

Reader 1: Why did he finish?

Reader 2: Who is the last man finishing the marathon, and why did he persist?

Reader 3: Why keep going when all is lost?

WHEN THE OTHER PERSON IS RIGHT

Reader 1: What did Barbara Walters do?

Reader 2: Why did Barbara Walters break down and go on the Carson show?

Reader 3: Can bad feelings between friends be resolved?

Are your questions close to any of these? Whether they are or not, you've earned 100 percent on this quiz! You see, there are no wrong answers: *It makes a difference how a story is told; it makes a difference how a story is heard.* Although I wrote all three stories myself, I'm sure that if I read them again a year from today, I'd find myself asking different questions than I am right now. That's okay. We grow and change and bring different things to each story every time we hear it. This chapter has been designed to help you improve your ability to *make* a story. In succeeding chapters, I'm going to show you how to more effectively *tell* a story. Remember, tension happens in real life; tension is artificially created in a story. And how do we do that? By asking or implying a question up front. Whenever we answer that question, the tension ends and we discover something.

Here are four more One-Minute Stories that illustrate the importance of tension and discovery. You'll discover that each involves a famous person, but you'll also discover inspiration in their triumphs over poverty, adversity, or just plain fear.

WHAT DO YOU NEED?

I have a friend who was so poor as a young boy that he was shuttled like a package among relatives. His only bed was two chairs pulled together. His clothes were always hand-me-downs.

When he'd stay with his grandmother, though, he'd listen for the whistles of distant trains. He would imagine himself in one of their fine cars. He spoke a lot with his grandmother, and one night she told him, "I don't think you'll be satisfied till you can climb to the top of the highest mountain and shout for all the world to hear, 'What do you need?'"

Though she didn't live to see it, she was right. In time

her grandson became world-famous, renowned not only as one of this century's great entertainers but also as the leader of an arduous, often frustrating battle against diseases that cripple children.

My friend is Jerry Lewis. When you watch him next Labor Day, listen closely. He's still asking, "What do you need?"

DECISION OF A LIFETIME

She was sixteen, an honors student—and she was trapped.

Her stepfather—whom she never seemed to please—not only did not encourage her studies, he also forbade her to participate in school activities.

Thus, when he found out that she had won the lead role in her high school play, he gave her a choice: Quit the play or get out of the house. What could she do?

Years later she told me that her hurt at that time was so great it had a color: deep purple.

At the worst of it, though, her mother and some friends came through. They helped her to leave home, and she did star in the school play.

Millions would come to know her as Melanie in *Gone With the Wind* and many other roles. She became a star and won two Academy Awards.

Yet the most challenging role for the incomparable Olivia de Havilland may have been performed before a far smaller audience—in a high school many years ago.

"I AM NOT MARLON BRANDO"

Because he wanted to act, day after day, week after week, year after year, he made every open casting call he could, hoping: "Maybe this time." Though rejected repeatedly, he would not quit. Agents refused to see him. Receptionists asked him time and again to sign their long yellow legal pads. Once, to see if it really mattered, he scribbled down the name of another actor, Marlon Brando. And no one noticed.

He joined a play in St. Louis. It failed, and he returned to New York, heartbroken. All along, he had supported his family by working as a substitute teacher. "Now," he thought, "maybe I'd better teach full-time."

But then another actor, Burgess Meredith, cast him in a play. Some folks from Hollywood noticed. He began appearing in movies and went on to star in a pair of hit television series, *All in the Family* and *Heat of the Night*.

Carroll O'Connor is no overnight success.

WHERE DOES PRESSURE COME FROM?

A famous fellow once told me that most talk about pressure is hogwash. Pressure, he said, comes from the inside—not from the outside—and it stems from a fear of failure.

He even volunteered an example:

"It's the seventh game of the World Series, and we're winning 3 to 2 in the bottom of the ninth. They have the bases loaded, two outs. Their best hitter is up. How's that?

"If we've all done our jobs right, every player on the field is saying to himself, 'I want that ball hit to *me*! I'm going to react just as I've practiced it a thousand times. *Please* hit it to *me*!'

"If instead a player says to himself, 'Geez, if it's hit to me and I miss it, we'll lose the game and the Series,' what's he really doing? He's creating pressure, because he's thinking about failing. You see, only when the player thinks positively can he deal with his fear of failing."

Tommy Lasorda, who managed the Los Angeles Dodgers for two decades, knows the game.

And baseball too.

9

How to Use a Story

Whether you have an audience of one or an audience of one hundred million—whether you're telling a joke to a friend or accepting your party's nomination for high office at a political convention—the same two rules apply:

1. **Pick a story for your audience.**
2. **Pick a story you like.**

To illustrate, here are two One-Minute Stories for you:

INTO THE STORM

He was a timid child, and his greatest fear was water. He was terrified by it—particularly dark or angry water.

Then one night when he was a young man, he walked to the shore of Lake Michigan during a great, rampaging storm. He stood there as the waves crashed at his feet. He vowed, "I can't turn my back on this. I have to face my fear."

He surely did.

In the years to come, he would scuba dive on camera, ride killer whales, sail across the Pacific Ocean. He'd fly planes and gliders too, drive a race car, trek across Antarctica.

That timid little boy has become one of America's most noted risk-takers and one of its most popular citizens. But, ironically, Hugh Downs's most courageous adventure was not captured on film: the night he walked into a storm.

STAY IN THE GAME

When the speeding car struck the beautiful young woman as she crossed the street, it tossed her body twenty feet into the air, like a sack of potatoes. Her skull was split. The doctors said she'd die. She survived that gloomy diagnosis, though she did have to wear a large cast for more than a year.

In time, she became the first woman executive to lead a major film studio. When she resigned at Paramount three years later, Hollywood pundits—like those doctors—said she was finished.

Then she produced a hit film called *Fatal Attraction*, once more confounding the experts.

When I asked this very talented, courageous woman—Sherry Lansing—why she hadn't given up, she told me:

"Everybody fails. Everybody takes his knocks, but the highly successful keep coming back. They stay in the game."

Hugh Downs and Sherry Lansing illustrate the power of the fourth of the Seven Steps to Self-Fulfillment:

THE FOURTH STEP
TO SELF-FULFILLMENT

1. Know who is responsible.

    Accept personal responsibility for your behavior. When you say, "I am responsible," you can build a new life, even a new world.
2. Believe in something big.

    Your life is worth a noble motive.
3. Practice tolerance.

    You will like yourself a lot more, and so will others.
4. **Be brave.**

    Remember, courage is acting *with* fear, not without it. If the challenge is important to you, you're supposed to be nervous.

Courage is acting with fear, not without it. One of the most dangerous misconceptions today, particularly among young people, is the false notion that somehow bravery means the absence of fear.

Sherry Lansing suggests, "I don't think that most people really understand the anxiety and doubts that very successful people have. The myth is that the successful are never insecure. The truth is that most of them are highly insecure, but they use their insecurity as a motivating factor. Because they want to overcome their anxieties, they push themselves twice as hard."

Hugh Downs is an excellent example. When I asked him one day about personal bravery, about the incredible risks he seems to take, he called himself a "devout coward," then went on to explain: "To give ourselves the best chance for success with any risk, we must prepare well. I've always been that way about aviation, for example. I really stack the cards in my favor. Some people laugh when I go through a checklist, it's so thorough. I have no death wish. I check everything. I've seen pilots come to grief because they skipped the details: Good preparation reduces anxiety—and the odds."

That's solid advice, isn't it?

When you make a plan, when you focus on solutions, you are in control. Your anxiety, fear, and anger become allies that can help you. Don't forget, if the challenge is important to you, you're supposed to be nervous:

Courage is acting *with* fear, not without it.

All right, now let's add a third rule to the two I gave you earlier for storytelling:

THREE FUNDAMENTAL RULES FOR STORYTELLING

1. **Pick a story for your audience.**
2. **Pick a story you like.**
3. *Practice your pick.*

If you choose your story for the two right reasons and earnestly rehearse telling the tale—again, whether it's meant as a joke told to a friend or in a speech before thousands—you will dramatically increase its impact. In Chapter 18, I'll suggest how to structure an entire talk. Before we get to that, though, I'd like you to do an exercise.

I've found in storytelling that sometimes it's a little easier to rehearse and see how tension is created in a different format.

For example, let's examine how to use a story to make a more compelling introduction. You'll recognize the two stories that follow, but note that a minor change has been made at the end of each:

INTO THE STORM

He was a timid child, and his greatest fear was water. He was terrified by it—particularly dark or angry water.

Then one night when he was a young man, he walked to the shore of Lake Michigan during a great, rampaging storm. He stood there as the waves crashed at his feet. He vowed, "I can't turn my back on this. I *have* to face my fear."

He surely did.

In the years to come, he would scuba dive on camera, ride killer whales, sail across the Pacific Ocean. He'd fly planes and gliders too, drive a race car, trek across Antarctica.

That timid little boy has become one of America's most noted risk-takers and one of its most popular citizens. And he's with us tonight.

Ladies and gentlemen, please join me in welcoming . . . Hugh Downs.

STAY IN THE GAME

When the speeding car struck the beautiful young woman as she crossed the street, it tossed her body twenty feet into the air, like a sack of potatoes. Her skull was split. The doctors said she'd die. She survived that gloomy diagnosis, though she did have to wear a large cast for more than a year.

In time, she became the first woman executive to lead a major film studio. When she resigned at Paramount three years later, Hollywood pundits—like those doctors—said she was finished.

Then she produced a hit film called *Fatal Attraction*, once more confounding the experts.

When I asked this very talented, courageous woman why she didn't give up, she told me: "Everybody fails. Everybody takes his knocks, but the highly successful keep coming back. They stay in the game."

And she has. Ladies and gentlemen, please join me in welcoming . . . Sherry Lansing.

You build tension in an introduction by withholding the subject's name until the last line.

If you create an introduction so that a person's name is not said until the last few words of the welcome—whether he or she is famous or not—you build tension. Not only does it usually make for a more interesting introduction when you delay disclosing the name, as a practical matter it also gives you the chance to lead the audience in applause the first time the name is announced, thus guaranteeing that your speaker or honored guest will be warmly received.

It's agonizing to be introduced in silence. It may be only three steps to the podium—but when it's quiet in the room, that's a lonnnnnnng three steps.

And speaking of silence, I'd like you to be familiar with one of the most important aspects of effective speaking:

When I asked my friend Jerry Lewis why—after seeing him perform countless times—I still laugh when he tells a joke whose punch line I already know, he replied: "It's not the joke that makes you laugh, it's the *timing*."

The advice Jerry gave me on timing, when I was rehearsing for Ford's Theatre in 1992, was to slow down. "Time is different onstage," he said, and I quickly found out how right he was: Even a second feels a lot longer to the performer than to anyone in the audience—and every performer discovers that a pause onstage seems to last forever. Yet, pauses are critical to effective speaking—because *pauses command our attention*.

The loudest sound in the English language is silence.

CHALLENGE NO. 10: PAUSE FOR EFFECT

I think you'll enjoy all three parts to this assignment. First, read aloud—slowly—"Into the Storm" and "Stay in the Game" as though you were introducing Hugh Downs and Sherry Lansing. This assignment works best if you can talk into a tape recorder, then review your work. Most important, practice pausing for two or three seconds at various places in each story.

For example, "He was a timid child [PAUSE], and his greatest fear was water." Or, "He was a timid child, and his greatest fear [PAUSE] was water." You might try, "He [PAUSE] was a timid child, and his greatest fear was water." Have fun with this. Don't hesitate to try a pause anywhere you'd like—but be sure that when you reach the last sentence of each One-Minute Story, you say it at least once *with* and once *without* a pause: "Please join me in welcoming [PAUSE] Hugh Downs." "Please join me in welcoming Hugh Downs."

Second, I'd like you to watch some funny folks—stand-up comics. You might choose late-night talk shows or comedy specials or a comedy channel. Or, if you can make the time, visit a comedy club. Wherever and whenever, study the timing of the funniest stand-up comics you can find. *Note their pauses*. You'll discover that very few actually tell jokes or stories. Instead, routines usually are a structured series of set-up lines and punch lines:

The comic, observing the sparsely filled auditorium, remarks:

SET-UP: *"Wow, this must be a wealthy city."*
[PAUSE]
PUNCH: *"I see each of you bought four or five seats."*

Third, over the next seven days, whenever humanly possible, consciously insert pauses in your conversations—and observe carefully the responses of your listeners. Insert pauses at work, with your family, at the dry cleaners, in the department store—every chance you get. It helped me to learn to stretch pauses by counting numbers in my head—"one, two, three"—whenever I paused. Now, don't shy away from this part of the assignment. I know that this exercise, more than any other, will help you feel the incredible power of silence—how a well-placed pause can grab and hold someone's attention. Please don't fret about getting it "right." Just do it.

10

Why Am I So Angry?

Let's review a paragraph from the beginning of Chapter 1:

The Confidence Course, anchored in practical life experience, will work for you because we *can* transform ourselves. The truth is, you and I define who we are every day by the choices we make, and thus, we choose who we want to be. I create myself. So do you. I invent myself. You do too. You and I are not what we eat; we are what we *think.* Confidence, by definition, is an attitude—and your attitude toward people and situations, just like mine, is subject to change. You're going to learn here how to swap one set of perceptions for another. The world will remain the same; how you *see* the world will be different.

When I asked you to listen closely to the language of others as part of Challenge No. 2: Not to Try, I'm sure you were able to see how sharply their words limited or expanded their world: The expression "I cannot" closed the door forever, didn't it? "I have not been able to," on the other hand, left choices.

The title *The Confidence Course* represents a similar choice of language. Why did I choose it? I first heard the expression from a drill instructor at Parris Island, South Carolina, in the fall of 1961. "The Confidence Course," he earnestly explained, was a succession of obstacles—logs, lines, and muddy water—that I, like the rest of our platoon of Marine recruits, was expected to conquer. The sergeant was both persuasive and determined that all of us would, in fact, master the course. He was very confident that we would succeed.

He was right. With his encouragement, we bested the beast. What did I learn from shinnying up ropes, leaping onto and over logs? For one, the Marine Corps was right to call the test a *confidence* course and not an *obstacle* course—because, truly, that was its purpose: "If I can get over that log, I can do anything." On that day, obstacles were an opportunity for some young recruits to gain confidence; every day, *obstacles are an opportunity to gain confidence.*

Every time we prevail—if even for a moment—over anxiety, fear of failure, feelings of vulnerability and inferiority, we are not left even. We are not as we were; we are ahead. With each obstacle we conquer, we grow larger. Consider again the lessons from your diary: Didn't the experience cause you to switch one set of perceptions for another? The world was the same; it was your attitude that changed.

*   *   *

Now we're going to examine how our attitudes and opinions form and sometimes get in our way. As my old drill instructor might say, it's easier to overcome an obstacle you can see. We'll also look at another powerful emotion—anger—what it is and what we can do with it. And we'll go further with storytelling, this time focusing on some simple, easy-to-learn devices to grab and hold someone's attention.

To grow in confidence, it's useful, of course, to recognize how we've come to see the world as we do—to see ourselves, to see others. Proceed with caution, though. What you're about to read could be more challenging, and disturbing, to you than any other passage in *The Confidence Course*. Why? Because I'll be asking you again to weigh just how deeply the old, familiar ways are ingrained in your personality—and this effort, like surgery, may hurt before it helps.

In 1965, when I returned home from Vietnam, I saw my country torn by opposing attitudes toward that war— two groups adamantly perceiving the same "evidence" in entirely different ways. Three decades later, in 1995, I and millions of other Americans again witnessed a searing national split over "evidence"—when the former football star O. J. Simpson was tried and ultimately acquitted of murder.

If you were old enough to form an opinion in 1965, what did you feel at the time about the Vietnam War?

Why?

In 1995, what did you feel about the jury's verdict that O. J. Simpson had not murdered his ex-wife and her friend? Why?

Do you feel strongly? I'm sure you recognize that those people who have a view different from yours believe just as strongly that they are right. How do we come to this? How can two people or two groups of people see the same event—and witness the same facts or evidence—so differently?

We *learn*.

Picture your mind as a doorway. At first, the opening is as wide as can be. We give you some information, though, and the door closes slightly. We give you a little more, and the door closes further. Somebody asks you a question about what you've learned—thereby encouraging you to commit to a position—and the door is left only slightly ajar, if open at all. You have begun to accept information that supports your point of view, and you've begun to reject information that challenges your point of view. You, my friend, have formed an attitude.

All attitudes, whether as corrosive as hate or as expansive as love, are the outcome of the same process. And that process is *learning*. We reflect attitudes, for example, when no one can persuade us to surrender our freedom or make us believe we are unworthy of respect.

Inevitably, our attitudes flavor our behavior. If we prefer one political party, we'll probably find ourselves more tolerant of the unique and differing characteristics of its members. "These are our people," we might say. On the other hand, the peccadilloes of individuals in opposing parties are sure targets of scorn.

We see what we believe we see.

Thus the anorexic, who is wafer-thin, sees herself as fat; the pretty movie starlet declares, "I'm ugly," when she notices a single pimple on her cheek; the weightlifter sighs and says, "I'm weak," because he fails to lift an incredible burden. In contrast, when the child described in the following One-Minute Story was confronted by obstacles, she saw a way out and up:

THE LITTLE GIRL WHO COULD

The little girl lived with her sister and grandmother in a tiny, disheveled room in a building at the corner of Yucca and Wilcox in Los Angeles, only a block from the famous Hollywood Boulevard.

Her parents, who lived apart, were both alcoholics. Her grandmother could be called, well, eccentric. Life was often noisy, confusing, and unpredictable for this little girl.

She found, though, that she could escape when the world became too unpleasant, that she could close her eyes and, through her imagination, travel to a better place—a land of fantasy where she could be whoever she wanted to be. "I am . . . ," she'd think—and she was!

Wonderfully, though, her real life would become larger than her greatest fantasy. And today Carol Burnett—a world-class talent and person—is one of America's most beloved stars.

Carol Burnett is an original—and so are you. I share her story with you for inspiration, not imitation. Can you imagine how different Carol's life would have been had she allowed the challenges of her childhood to dictate her choices? Carol found a way out and up. You can too.

What is confidence? Confidence is an attitude.

CHALLENGE NO. 11: ENVISION

If you had to choose one opinion of yours that might cause discomfort to you or to someone else, which would it be? One student told me that she always expected men to be more decisive than women. Another student described his intense feelings about racial differences, which he said he knew were wrong and irrational and made him ashamed. A third talked about how low an opinion she had of herself, and she summed up her thoughts with this question: "How can I get over the fear of being alone and responsible for myself after a lifetime of others caring for me?"

Here's the assignment: I would like you to make some quiet time for yourself; lie back and picture how you would behave if you believed differently. What would your behavior be like if you held an opposite opinion? (How would the last student, for example, act in a given situation if she were not frightened?) There's a second part to this exercise, which will come later, in Challenge No. 15. For now, take your time—sleep on it if you'd like—and remember to envision yourself in action.

How angry are you?

I was angry, *predisposed* to be angry, for most of my early adult years. Although I was unaware of how deeply I had been scarred, the anger and violence I had endured as a child had prepared me to see the world—*to anticipate the behavior of others*—through a tightly focused lens. My choices were far narrower than I knew. Never was this more apparent than one night more than two decades ago as I walked with my wife, Loretta, on a Manhattan street:

My wife, who was seven months pregnant with our second child, had to walk more slowly than most of the other hockey fans streaming out of Madison Square Garden. It was an unusually warm night in 1974, and the crowd had thinned by the time we turned the corner a block from our car and I spotted danger.

Ahead of us was a group of four or five teenagers who were throwing karate kicks and punches at one another. They crowded the narrow sidewalk and seemed oblivious to any passerby who could be hurt by their noisy horseplay. As we neared them, I began to hear my heart beat. I glanced at my pregnant wife. *No one,* I thought, *no one is going to touch my wife.* The heat rose along my spine and into my neck. My heart pumped faster, my breathing quickened, my jaw tightened. No longer was I a thoughtful newspaper editor. I was a seven-year-old boy who, with blood flowing down his face, wouldn't surrender his Bonomo's Turkish Taffy to two street bullies; I was a fifteen-year-old who knew how to throw a straight right hand; I was a twenty-one-year-old Marine sergeant in Vietnam. I would protect our unborn child. Within a few feet of the teenagers, I stepped forward quickly and placed my hands on the shoulders of two of them, tightened my fingers, drew them to me, then spread them apart. "Cool it," I said, my voice hard and ugly. The teenagers looked at one another, said nothing, stepped aside, and let us pass.

When we reached our car and entered it, my heart continued to pound and my forehead was moist. I started to tremble.

Loretta reached across the seat, clasped my hand, and said, "We could have crossed the street."

I sat quietly, my hands falling loosely from the steering wheel. I was confused. Did I do the right thing? It had never entered my mind to cross the street. I watched the teenagers pass by, and they no longer looked threatening; they were just kids. *We could have crossed the street.* What if they had been armed? I had endangered my wife and myself. Why did I *choose* violence?

A few minutes later, as we drove up the FDR Drive in silence, I said softly, "You're right."

11

Moving Beyond Anger

Anger is the child of frustration. We are not born angry. We learn it—almost immediately. Moreover, anger and violence make no class distinctions. At every level of society, unchecked anger has provoked violent outbursts, assaults and biting insults, murder and suicide. It has caused or aggravated physical problems like headaches, high blood pressure, heart attacks, and ulcers. It's often concealed in complaining and whining. It's even possible, as many psychiatrists think, that a crippling emotional condition like depression sometimes is *suppressed* anger.

When we were infants, our desires were quickly satisfied, but it wasn't long before we were encouraged to adjust to the will of others and to live with the frustration of not having our own way. We learned to eat and sleep on a schedule assigned by others. We were forced to use strange utensils to eat with, although our fingers worked just fine. Even our bladders had to be disciplined. In succeeding years we had to learn to adapt more and more to school, to work, to the demands of someone else. Countless times we have been assured that controlling our temper is a measure of our maturity. Is it any wonder, then, that we frequently conceal or even deny our anger?

As important as exercising restraint is, however, it's only half the story. While we diligently study anger's ugliness—and we will continue to examine its dangers later in this chapter—we often neglect to recognize its positive side: Anger can be an affirmation that we exist, that we care.

"Why am I so angry?"

Asking the question begins the process of making anger, like anxiety, an ally in our lives. Anger can help us improve, can motivate us to achieve noble goals, and—most important—can be an invaluable alarm system in our day-to-day lives. Anger is, after all, a form of *energy*. Properly directed, this energy can alert us to legitimate concerns; it can give us the needed push to face some of life's most difficult challenges.

When the citizen pounds his fist at the town board meeting and raises his voice to decry injustice, he's really shouting that he's concerned, that he's willing to say it aloud, that he's willing to overcome his own fear of expressing his anger, that he believes strongly that good can result.

Anger gets things done. It's the energy that inspires creative acts. Anger is the push that moves you to demand a raise, the burst that sends the depleted athlete sprinting across the finish line, the nudge that moves you to find a better job or a better life.

How do we make anger work for us?

First, admit you're angry. Sound easy? Often we deny it even to ourselves, especially when it seems coldly selfish or irrational. The unfettered anger a small boy may exhibit at his mother's death ("She left me alone—I hate her!") is easier to comprehend than the frustration we feel when a boss doesn't treat us like one of the family or we must wait in line. More than simply saying the words, feel them: "I am angry!"

Second, analyze the anger. What is the frustration? When you're stuck in a traffic jam, the problem is out of your control; it's out there on the road, and there's nothing you can do about it. When your feelings are hurt because your teacher doesn't treat you as if she were your mother, ask yourself, "Is my anger appropriate?" Be honest; this is a toughie. The answer could end your anger. On the other hand, if you're denied a promotion because of sex, race, age, or nationality, your anger is appropriate—and useful.

Third, deal with the anger. If you're in a traffic jam, you're stuck. Acceptance is your answer, because that's all you can do about it. That's when all those lessons about controlling your temper have value. Take a deep breath. Relax. No one else is moving either. If, however, you've been unfairly denied a promotion, anger is ready to work for you. The adrenaline is flowing, the blood is rushing— you've never been more alert. Don't squander that precious energy agitating about the unfairness of your plight: "Oh, poor little me! How I suffer!" Instead, while your anger has you sharp, explore the possibilities and the opportunities. Should you quit or should you fight? If you choose the former, actively start your search. If you decide to fight, research how others in similar situations have succeeded—then proceed. *Focus on a solution*, and anger will be your ally.

Let me emphasize again the choices that anger affords us: We can sublimate that energy into positive activities like problem-solving, jogging, rearranging furniture, or working harder. We can create a sculpture or write a poem. Or we can vent the anger by kicking a chair, sulking, unfairly punishing a child, grumbling at coworkers, or picking on our spouse. But whatever we do, something happens to that energy—something we determine.

What we've been focusing on mainly is anger as a reaction to an immediate situation or frustration. Now let's take a look at another kind of anger: *chronic* anger, a *predisposition* to anger—in other words, the *attitude* of anger.

When I was a young adult, as the Madison Square Garden story illustrates, I was chronically angry—which means I was prepared to be angry at the slightest provocation. Fortunately, I have been able to change this attitude over the years. Had I been unwilling or unable to change, *The Confidence Course* would not exist. (At least, it certainly would not have been written by *me*!) Chronic anger, after all, is corrosive; it destroys lives.

Chronically angry people are judgmental, quick to see others as threats. They have an immense need to control. Sadly, even when they achieve control, it does not give them lasting satisfaction. This is also the description, of course, of a bully. So it's not surprising to hear chronically angry adults describe children, even their own, as defiant, pampered, immature, or spoiled—when, ironically, it is the chronically angry adults themselves who most exhibit a childlike inability to handle frustration. When I was a little boy and my grandmother advised me to avoid colds and angry people, unbeknownst to her, she was doing more than talking *to* me: She was talking *about* me.

Yes, *me*.

To transform myself, I had to admit a painful truth: I was an angry person. I also had to accept that I was responsible for who I was. (Now you know where the first of the Seven Steps to Self-Fulfillment comes from.) That understood, I was able to learn some things that I hope will be as helpful to you as they have been to me:

First, I *can* change. And so can you.

Next, I grasped the obvious: It's no fun to be angry. My anger made me uncomfortable. When I was angry, I experienced many of the same kinds of physical reactions that I did when I was anxious or afraid: racing heartbeat, higher blood pressure, a rush of adrenaline. To top it all, I did not like myself very much when I was angry—and almost always I was sorry later that I had gotten angry.

In time I began to realize that *he who angers you conquers you*. If I was furious at someone, for example, I couldn't sleep. My antagonist, on the other hand, slept like a baby. So, whom did my anger hurt?

Over the years, as I began to honestly examine what I had grown so angry about, I saw that my anger usually grew from one of two personal frustrations: Either I didn't think I'd be able to achieve some goal, or I felt I couldn't avoid an unpleasant circumstance. If I could not get something I wanted, accomplish some end, have my own way in a situation or control the behavior—even the thoughts—of other people, I became angry. Looking back, I was like the child bellowing stubbornly that he wants that toy in the window. What a hopeless, futile task I had taken on: to control the world around me. What I really needed to control, I slowly began to recognize, was *me*. I—and no one else—was responsible for how I felt: How I perceived a situation made my anger flare. Others didn't necessarily see what I saw. Worse, I was often downright wrong! It was I who didn't see that I could cross the street. Finally, it came to me:

Most of the time, anger is a choice.

If you have struggled—and suffered—with anger, as I have, I think you'll find useful these ten suggestions for handling some of life's more frustrating moments:

TEN WAYS TO MOVE BEYOND ANGER

1. **Time out.**
   Let time and distance separate you from the source of your frustration. A coworker was as hot-tempered as I was, but we needed each other for

either of us to succeed. How did we work it out? When one of us would grow too impatient, the other would raise his hand—and discussion of the topic ceased. When we could discuss the subject calmly, we'd start again. At first we looked like two students in a classroom trying to get the teacher's attention. Hands flew in the air. After a few weeks, though, the hands were raised less and less frequently. In a few months the hands were not raised at all—and neither of us mentioned it for a full year.

When you can, *walk away.* The adrenaline rush you feel will normally diminish or cease in about twenty minutes, particularly if you perform a physical activity like walking or exercising. So, take time out—and put your body in motion. Movement helps.

2. **Let it go.**
   Can you accommodate or compromise? Confident, intelligent adults do both. The question is not whether you should accommodate but whether you *can*. Are you a mule, or can you find an alternative? If you're inflexible, as was often the case with me, ask yourself whether you're fighting to hold on to your anger, insisting on control, or trying to solve a problem. Are you trying too hard to prove that your way is the only way? If you have an angry attitude, you're probably stubborn too.

   Let it go: You cannot only if you say you cannot.

3. **Negotiate.**

   Search for common ground. Keep the discussion on the issue at hand, not on personality. If you call the other person names or demean his behavior or opinion, mutual trust is lost. Don't kid yourself: If you get your way in a disagreement by ridiculing the other person, you've only convinced that person of your power *at the moment.* And you've made an adversary who, when she or he has the power and the opportunity, will fix your wagon.

   We tend to remember who hurt our feelings. Negotiate, don't manipulate. Ask yourself, "Am I sincerely speaking in the other person's interest, or am I only trying to justify my own position? Am I trying to discover the best way to resolve our difference, or am I trying to win?"

4. **Watch your language!**

   If you're speaking in extremes, using words like "never" or "always," knock it off. More often than not, extreme words are used as an implied threat: "I can never accept this!" If you use ominous, menacing, or threatening words, in one sense you will succeed: Your intent will be understood. And, like winning by intimidation when you call someone a name, every time you overwhelm another person, you can look forward to someday being paid back with interest. Most people have long memories, especially when they have to suppress humiliation to survive the moment. Also, as with the word "cannot," your language defines your world.

If you discipline yourself to search for positive, constructive words in situations, you will think positively and constructively: You are what you think.

5. **Listen.**

For one thing, you may be wrong. But you'll know that only if you quell your anger while you listen. Ask, "How can I better see this from his, her, or their point of view?" If you listen carefully, sometimes you'll find that there's a hidden agenda. When, for example, a child misbehaves to get attention, a loving parent examines the inappropriate behavior and the reasons behind it. We may tend to forget the profound truth in that understanding when we are adults—sometimes at great risk.

When one spouse becomes explosively furious at the other for a small oversight—he was a few minutes late for dinner—it's probably not the incident that's the problem but the perception that the lateness was another example of how he ignores her feelings. He would do well to listen carefully and uncover the real reasons for his wife's outburst; she would do well to express her real feelings. Both need to examine their behavior and the reasons behind it.

6. **Hug.**

Yes, I said *hug*. If you're angry at a loved one, hug that person. And mean it. You may not want to hug—which is all the more reason to do so. It's hard to stay angry when someone shows they love you, and that's precisely what happens when we hug each other. If you're angry in a situation in which a physical hug would be inappropriate behavior—you're in a pitched battle with a business colleague or a supervisor, for example—use *words* to hug: "Mary, I want you to know that your friendship [or leadership] is more important to me than this thing that has me [and you] so upset. I want you to know how much I appreciate and need your friendship [or leadership]. Do you think we could take a five-minute break? I need one. I'm sure I'll be able to see this more clearly—and certainly find a better way to share my concern—if we break for a couple of minutes."

7. **Apologize.**
As we explored in Chapter 7, mistakes are a natural and valuable part of life. When we attempt to hide our errors, we usually fail. Our anger festers: We resent questions about our behavior, and we grow self-righteous, defensive, and uncomfortable. Lighten up, my friend. Say, "I'm sorry," when you screw up. That simple admission will diminish your anger like a raindrop on a burning matchstick—only faster. More, when you sincerely apologize, you take responsibility for your actions: *You are in control.* As for who gets the last word in a disagreement that has you steaming at the gills, let the other guy have it. In fact, make that your noble goal: to be certain the other fellow gets the last word. *The only sure way to win a fight is to avoid one—and the only sure way to prolong a fight is to seek the last word.* Discussion is

a butterfly; argument is a sand flea. Which would you like at your picnic?

8. **Keep perspective.**

I've witnessed human catastrophe, thus I recognize that there's a world of difference between annoyance and trouble. Being a few minutes late, finding your jacket soiled, your faucet broken, or the wrong package delivered to your front door are annoyances. Facing terminal cancer, living with Alzheimer's or AIDS, the pain of war or poverty are troubles. Annoyance is bothersome; trouble is serious. Save your energy for the big stuff. Most of what angers us is only an annoyance.

To help keep perspective, it's always wise to ask: "What's the worst thing that can happen?"

9. **Make a plan.**

How are you going to deal with the anger-provoking person or situation? First, ask yourself: "What do I want to achieve?" (If your answer is "to hurt somebody," you're not ready to make a plan. Calm yourself: Take deep breaths, go for a walk, let some of that adrenaline dissolve. When you've settled down enough to see that the best goal is to resolve the situation—not to exact revenge for the hurt you feel or to injure others because you're angry—you can move forward.) Continue asking questions: "What do I need? Does a resolution require someone else's help? What steps can I take to solve the problem or relax the situation? What are my options? What reasonable accommodations can I make?"

Write down a plan. You'll be absolutely amazed at how much better this makes you feel: *You are in control.*

Sometimes a plan may be as simple as deciding on the words you'll use in an upcoming situation: Imagine what the others will say and how you'll respond. Keep in mind that your words should be chosen—scripted in advance, if you will—to lessen tension and to help keep everybody focused on finding a solution. If you think the other person might say, "I'm upset at what you did, because it hurt my feelings," prepare yourself in advance not to reply, "That's ridiculous." By thinking about it in advance, you'll recognize that the other person's declaration of hurt is an opportunity. So, express regret, accept responsibility for the part you played, and explore whether there's a way the two of you, working together, can prevent a recurrence.

Now let's get something out of the way: If you dismiss the sincere expression of another person, your real goal is to hurt, not heal. Don't let your anger do the talking. Planning will help you choose your words and thoughts more carefully. For example, if you think about it, you'll avoid saying, "Don't be angry." Telling someone who is angry not to be angry is a lot like telling someone who is frightened, "Don't be afraid." He already knows he doesn't like what he's feeling. Instead, *give him a reason to diminish his anger or fear.* That you can do.

If your anger arises from business—perhaps a

situation with another employee at work or a mistake on a telephone bill at home—decide whom you need to speak with, find out when that individual is available, gather what information or material you need to resolve the question, and determine the order in which you should act. Again, write it down: *Make a plan.*

10. **Ask for help.**

Depending upon your need, this ranges from friends and relatives to professional counselors. The good news is that, if you have an angry attitude—if you're as predisposed to flare up as I was—help is available. Seeking assistance is a sign of strength, maturity, and courage, not weakness. I know you'll be delighted—and probably surprised—by how many people, especially friends and relatives, are eager to help you if only you ask. Talking through your feelings with someone you trust not only makes you feel better, it also helps you get to the root of your anger. Do you remember the example I gave of the loving parents—how they responded to the child's behavior and the reasons behind it?

Be your own loving parent. Ask for help.

CHALLENGE NO. 12: YOUR ANGER LOG

As you did for your worries in Challenge No. 3, keep a similar journal now of the anger-provoking situations and people in your life. In other words, write down and describe the times you got angry. Log what happens, why you got angry, how it made you feel. If you do this for three or four weeks, we won't have to revisit it in *The Confidence Course*. You'll find that, although you won't be able to solve every problem that makes you angry, your confidence will grow—and your attitude will change.

12

How to Love—and Be Loved

We are not meant to live among strangers.

Socially and biologically, human beings are meant to live in small groups—families, clans, and tribes—and to know everyone from birth to death. I suspect we're far more like wolves and chimps than honeybees or ants. Yet our urban centers, where most of the planet's population resides, look more like bustling anthills or busy beehives than quiet villages: Who are all these people? *Is it any wonder that so many of us feel anxious, isolated, lonely? How can we trust someone we don't know?* Just maybe, the very idea of civilization—cities—is not natural.

If I'm right, how can any of us possibly endure in the complex, *civilized* world in which we live?

We can make friends.

And we can love.

*　　*　　*

In this chapter we're going to examine why we're drawn to love, how we give and receive love, how our various needs for love continue to evolve throughout all of our lives. We'll explore the essential differences between sex and love, and we'll take a close look at friendship and love.

I hope that you will be both reinforced and challenged by what you're about to read. *The Confidence Course* could not exist without suggesting how to love and be loved. And, because this is a real-life course, we'll look at those tender times when we must let go of someone we love—and how to get through the sorrow. In another sensitive area, we'll take a hard look at criticism: how to give it; how to receive it.

Perhaps a long, long time ago, it happened one day like this:

Although the fur pelts were wrapped in several layers, the biting-cold air seeped through to his body, and he shuddered. The ground was icy-hard, and the falling snow made it even more difficult to climb and to step over the stones, now slick and slippery with moisture. Determined not to fall, though, he made his way slowly, all the while holding the prize tightly to his side. It was *meat*, and it would sustain them. Finally, he reached the threshold. He pulled the protective hides aside and stepped stiffly through the cave entrance. Slowly, as he walked deeper into the dark recesses, the air grew warmer. He heard the baby before he saw her—and he smiled.

Why did he return? What brought him back?

I think it was love.

The impulse to love, I believe, is as compelling as any human drive. Let's take a closer look. In fact, let's contrast it with sex—the drive most widely associated with love: We know that sex, like hunger and self-preservation, is an instinct—but is love an instinct? I don't think so; I think love is something more, and I think we learn *how* to love. Instincts, by their very definition, are biological and difficult to suppress. We all know that love, unfortunately, can be suppressed and even extinguished.

Sex is stimulated by our glands; love incorporates our whole personality. Sex is biological; love is psychological. The human sex drive can be indiscriminate and stimulated by novelty; love, however, is extremely discriminating and seeks to be exclusive. Most important, sex may be interpreted by an attitude—but love *is* an attitude.

When children are raised in a healthy family, sex and love are kept separate. When a small boy from a loving family experiments with sex, the child's playmates in this exploration are not the people he most loves. Actually, it is not until adolescence—with touching, kissing, and petting—that these two strands of development, sex and love, begin to weld together so that later, as adults, we can enjoy healthy relationships.

How sex and love are blended in a mature adult parallels, of course, the three stages you studied earlier:

A child learns to trust; an adolescent searches for identity; adults see beyond themselves.

When we're children, we have an enormous need to be loved; but when we're adults, we develop another, even greater need:

We need *to* love.

You know you're in love when the joy and comfort of another person are as important to you as your own.

It has been said many times that to love another person we must first love ourselves. That's true—and it's a grown-up understanding. Said another way, to have confidence in someone else—to trust—we must first have confidence in ourselves.

To have a relationship with someone else, I must be able to say: "I commit to *you*. I believe in *you*. I believe in *us*." To truly commit to another person, however, I must know who I am and what I want out of life: *If I do not know who I am, how on earth can I recognize someone who is right for me?*

The adolescent answers the question quickly—too quickly: "All I want is *him* [or *her*]!" That's a delusion; we cannot find our identity in another person. "All I want is him" may sound romantic, but it's unrealistic. It's a hope based on expectations that almost certainly will be disappointed.

Before we go further, rest easy. I'm not about to diminish love or define it to death. On the contrary, we're going to look at it through a larger lens.

Do you remember your first love?

Our first love enlarges us. It inspires us. It occurs when we are free and the future is filled with promise. Usually it is physical, powerful, and profound. Our first love consumes us and makes all else irrelevant. It owns our time. We act as we think we should act, sometimes embarrassing ourselves. Like a hurricane, our first love—based in adolescence—normally doesn't last. And when the last raindrop falls and the gale becomes a breeze, what's left?

I hope it's friendship.

There is a lot of make-believe in many human relationships. We seek to achieve certain ends—like pleasing the boss or pleasing the customer, for example—so we act our best: *We want to be liked*. To keep others from thinking badly of us (to be liked), we often hide negative or hurtful feelings. We put on masks—and, sadly, some of us seek approval so desperately that we risk becoming as superficial as our masks. To have a friend means we can lay our masks aside: *We can be ourselves*. In fact, when we're with a real friend, we may be more able to be ourselves—to be free—than even when we are alone.

Friendships must be built over time; they are not static. When we "instantly" make a friend, it is a mirage, an illusion. Only time and testing build trust, which is the foundation of friendship:

ARE YOU MY FRIEND?

1. You give me time.
2. You listen to me—and you listen without making me feel judged.

3. You're quick to remind me that I have strengths.
4. You help me heal when I'm hurting.
5. You tell me the truth when it will help me; you don't tell me the truth when it won't help me.
6. You show me by your demeanor, tone, and smile that it's important to you that I feel secure, comfortable, at ease.
7. You show me that you're sorry when you hurt my feelings; you allow me to show you that I'm sorry when I hurt your feelings.
8. You don't abuse me. *Ever.* You make sure that I know you seek to protect me.
9. You make small surprises for me.
10. You find words that support the best that is in me.
11. You let me cry when I need to.
12. You encourage me to tell the truth to you and to admit when I'm afraid.

Yes, you are my friend. And I need you.

Sounds an awful lot like love, doesn't it?

CHALLENGE NO. 13: CULTIVATE FRIENDSHIPS

If you're fortunate enough to have one or more people like this in your life, do something before you read any further: Write a letter or call them now. Copy the list if you'd like, and share it. If you do not have such a friend yet, keep reading. This book is about getting there.

For many people in this century, a classic marriage includes love and sex between two adults. It assumes frequent and close contact between the partners and *friendship* as well as love. There's also an expectation of shared responsibility to build and nurture the marriage and the family.

This popular concept of marriage, as you're aware, is not so easy to achieve. In addition to the social stresses we seem to see hammered to death on television talk shows every weekday afternoon, there is biology at work here: Adolescents, for example, have a powerful sex drive years before they're ready to assume the real responsibilities of an adult relationship. Further, throughout their lives, normal men and women are able to find more than one person alluring. We can be aroused by and attracted to more than a single individual—which, of course, does not make monogamy a walk along the beach. No one needs to take *The Confidence Course* to discover that a large number of marriages end in divorce.

So, aside from abusive relationships, what do I believe are the most frequent causes of marital discord?

Unreasonable expectations—and a failure to communicate.

If we expect our partner and our children to be flawless, we're going to be disappointed. Worse, tension increases with unreasonable expectations.

When partners cease to talk honestly with each other—even when, at first, it's to avoid hurt feelings or to prevent an angry exchange—an uneasy truce occurs. It may seem safe, even smart, but it is peace at a price.

Why do I believe that such silence—this "truce"— destroys a relationship?

Because, as I suggested earlier, we're most at ease when we're with someone we trust—when we can be ourselves, unguarded, not tiptoeing on eggshells. If we don't share our fears and anxieties with our partner—the friend at home—then with whom do we share them? Few things hurt as much as not being able to share your feelings—to talk—with the person you love. Not communicating is a sure way to arouse resentment, then hurt.

Folks hurt each other when they're unable to tell each other how they really feel. It's possible that at least some extramarital affairs are conducted expressly to be discovered—to force discussion of the unsaid. In the troubled marriages I've witnessed, the most common complaints have been, "My partner is thoughtless, selfish, and he [or she] takes me for granted."

A failure to communicate.

While love is an important ingredient of a successful marriage, a relationship based solely on romance will experience difficulty, because a marriage is meant to be lasting while a romance is fleeting. Romance happens; marriages are built.

Whether a couple is married or not, a relationship must be active to last. Human beings are meant to grow, not stagnate:

By the choices we make, we grow larger or we become smaller every day.

What, precisely, is growth?

146

It is overcoming doubt, gaining confidence. Every human being struggles. *Our lover cannot remove our struggle.* Each of us, alone, is responsible for his own behavior and must conquer his own doubts; but a loving partner reinforces us, helps to strengthen us. A loving partner sees the best in us, the best we can be, and encourages us. (He or she is growing too.)

Again, however, until I know who I am and what I want, I cannot know who or what is best for me.

If I am not committed to my own growth, how can I be committed to someone else's?

Often, particularly when we're young, we look for the ideal mate. That's not surprising for an adolescent, is it? The adolescent, searching for identity, asks: "Who am I?" It stands to reason: If my partner is perfect, aren't I perfect? Intoxicated with love, the adolescent sees her sweetheart as ideal (who that person *could* be), not real (who that person is). As I said earlier, our first love occurs when we are free and the future is filled with promise.

We can miss the passion, the eroticism, and the romanticism as we age—and, unfortunately, confuse it with losing our youth. I've seen men in their middle years fly upside down, act like adolescents, and ascribe to their youth precisely what they find missing in their lives now. As if a dormant seed of adolescence suddenly sprouted in their middle years, they long for the passion, the promise, the person to inspire them.

They're as vulnerable as the adolescents they used to be and, again, they miss the shortcomings: *We see what we believe we see.* Like the teenagers they once were, they blaze with love. But let a negative comment, a criticism from their new "ideal person" or a put-down occur—and reality bites. They plunge to earth: "How," they wonder, "did I ever see this person as perfect for me?"

What have they missed?

It is the relationship, not the person, that must be made ideal.

Before my son, Eric, and my daughter-in-law, Claudia, were married, I advised them: "We get married at the worst possible time—when we're in love."

We're dazzled, I said: Our passions stoked, we can't see straight. We're infatuated, and we overlook behavior that in someone else we'd find objectionable. But time has a way of clearing our vision. Within a year and a half, we *will* notice what we don't like: "No, honey, I don't think so." "Hey, how come we don't talk anymore?" "Do you have to spend so much?" "If I knew you were this selfish . . . "

If you're like nearly every other normal human being, some of your passion will subside. Time does that. When our blood is rushing, it seems impossible that the exhilaration can ever diminish—but it will. And it's okay. You see, that's when a life of love can really begin. With the fever down, we're free to choose:

If you become friends, your love can last a lifetime.

Liz Smith, the popular newspaper columnist, once told me: "I was extremely involved with love and romance when I was younger, and I rushed like a mad person trying to resolve my conflicts. But now I think the greatest thing that has happened to me are the wonderful friends I've made along the way. They are people I can really count on. This is the love that's really important. I had to be older, to have lived my life, to come to this truth. I was very involved with romantic love for years, but I don't think romantic relationships, as exciting as they are at first, last as we might wish. The great marriages, I believe, are those in which the partners become friends."

Like Liz, I respect the relationship between friendship and love, *when the joy and comfort of another person are as important to me as my own.* Sex in and of itself is not love, and neither is saying, "I love you." Of course, sex can be a joyous expression of love, a communication, as can the beautiful words "I love you." Actually, that's what is felt and heard by those people among us who choose to see beyond themselves. We call these people adults.

I believe love is so important, it is the fifth of the Seven Steps to Self-Fulfillment:

THE FIFTH STEP TO SELF-FULFILLMENT

1. Know who is responsible.
   Accept personal responsibility for your behavior. When you say, "I am responsible," you can build a new life, even a new world.
2. Believe in something big.
   Your life is worth a noble motive.

3. Practice tolerance.

You will like yourself a lot more, and so will others.

4. Be brave.

Remember, courage is acting *with* fear, not without it. If the challenge is important to you, you're supposed to be nervous.

5. **Love someone.**

Because you should know joy.

13

The Abuse of Love

It would be far easier for me to skip ahead right now than to discuss the next topic, which is the abuse of love. I lived in fear as a child and, because of my personal experience, I am especially sensitive to the subject. I know from teaching *The Confidence Course*, however, that this section is critically important for many students and should be included. If you have been hurt, I hope this helps. If you have not been hurt, I hope you learn something in this passage that will enable you to help someone who has been a victim—and will discourage you if *you* are ever in a position where you have the power to make someone a victim.

Emotional abuse is "the systematic diminishment of another," says the New York attorney Andrew Vachss, a man who has devoted his life to protecting children. "It may be intentional or subconscious—or both—but it is always a course of conduct, not a single event. It is designed to reduce a child's self-concept to the point where the victim considers himself unworthy—unworthy of respect, unworthy of friendship, unworthy of the natural birthright of all children: love and protection."

It is a nightmare: It is abuse of a parent's power. It is abuse of love.

The abuser bullies and demeans the child's efforts: "Can't you do anything right?" The abuse can include physical pain—but the deeper, lasting wound is emotional: The child is encouraged to believe "I'm no good."

Some years after I had served in Vietnam, I was amazed at how readily my fellow Americans who had never served in a war accepted the diagnosis that veterans can suffer "post-traumatic stress syndrome"—what soldiers in earlier wars called "shell shock" or "combat fatigue." Yet it seems so difficult for many of the same people to grasp the fact that the abuse of a child's love has the same consequences— and those consequences can last a lifetime. The abused child is the victim of a war as surely as the fellow who is awarded a Purple Heart. The truth is, Marines in war fight more for one another than they fight for flag or country. In combat, they have each other for support—but who is more alone than an abused child?

When my father got drunk and beat me when I was a boy, I'd say later, "I wish I hadn't made Daddy so mad."

My words, it's easy to see today, were those of a victim.

I would try to "explain" what my father did to me by assuming the blame—the guilt—for my own abuse. In hindsight, of course, I know now that I wasn't responsible for what my father did to me; he alone was responsible for his behavior.

Inevitably, though, victims are made to feel guilty—made to believe, paradoxically, that the abuse they suffer is somehow *their* fault:

No one ever has the right to abuse you, whether you are a child or an adult.

When I asked Andrew Vachss one day to define the difference between sick and evil, he told me, "When a pedophile lusts for a child, that's sick. When the pedophile touches the child, that's evil."

On the one hand, most adults who were victims as children do not become abusers as adults—although they are experts at abusing themselves. On the other hand, it's extremely rare for an adult who's an abuser not to have been abused as a child.

A television talk-show host once speculated that I would not have had the success I've enjoyed if I had not been wounded as a child. I told her the truth: "I am who I am today *despite* my childhood, not because of it." If we toss a handful of seeds onto a concrete sidewalk, one seed—despite all odds—may take root and a flower bloom. Imagine, though, the flowers we'd have if that same seed were planted in fertile soil and nurtured. *Every* child deserves somebody to be crazy about them, to nurture them.

Abuse is always wrong.

Some parents, who should not be parents at all, do something particularly pernicious: They withhold their love until their children "earn" it. These children are made to fulfill their parents' unreasonable demands. For such youngsters, life is a never-ending, futile quest to make their parents "proud"—to *perform* as their parents insist. Unlike the children of truly loving parents, these children face a range of challenges that can include, in one home, pathologically strict standards; in another home, responsibility for "caring for" their parents; and in yet another home, violations of labor laws, drug abuse, and prostitution. Often they're forced to be little adults, not allowed to be children.

You may know adults who've been raised in such households; they constantly seek approval. I've known famous stage performers who confused applause from an audience—*approval*—with love. That's probably why, when our daughter, Melinda, was a young teenager and had an opportunity to model and to perform onstage professionally, her mother and I suggested that she decline. She followed our advice, and years later, as I was writing *The Confidence Course,* Melinda reminded me of what we had told her: "You said young models and actresses tend to confuse affection with attention."

Whenever a powerful corporate executive, a senior military officer, or a high public official abuses a subordinate, he or she is a predator, using the power of the position to create a victim. It is what it looks like—it is abuse—and it feels like abuse. The attention is not affection; in fact, the abuser fails to see the other person as a person.

Well, what do we do?

First, we tightly embrace number one of the Seven Steps to Self-Fulfillment: "I am responsible for my behavior." Next, we accept that we are not responsible for our abuser's behavior. And we admit to ourselves the most important truth of all: We do not deserve to be abused—which, of course, is exactly the lie every abuser tries to sell. "Honey, don't you know how much I love you? You shouldn't have said what you said. Can't you see? I get mad, baby, because I'm crazy about you."

Should you forgive?

That's up to you.

Forgiving doesn't mean that the abusive behavior is excused. Forgiving *does* mean that, first, you admit you have been hurt; second, you accept responsibility, if any, for exposing yourself to hurt; and third, you tell the person who hurt you that you no longer hurt. (The second step is not to suggest that a victim should assume responsibility for the abuse but to encourage the victim to look for an exit and, when possible, use it.) I believe that if you take the third step—actually decide to forgive—it should be to release yourself from your own anger and not to free from guilt the person who hurt you. A counselor who tells victims that they must forgive their abusers in order to heal themselves is, in my opinion, further abusing the victims.

You are not responsible for your abuser's rehabilitation.

Whether you decide to forgive is up to you alone. No one

has the right to insist that you forgive. I've never heard this truth expressed better than in a summation Andrew Vachss gave to one jury: "The right belongs to the wronged."

CHALLENGE NO. 14: SEE YOURSELF AS YOU'D LIKE TO BE

Reread the passage about chronic anger in Chapter 11 and see how it relates to what you've just read about abuse, then ask yourself: "Does any of this apply to me or to someone I know? Am I frustrated? Am I angry? Am I sad or depressed? Have I been abused? Could my own behavior be described as abusive?"

Whether or not you've answered "yes" to any of the questions, write down on a piece of paper what you'd really like to change right now about yourself or your situation: How would you like your life to be different? Assume for this exercise that there's no reason you cannot have—or be—all you desire. What do you need? What would you like to do?

After you've completed the written part of this assignment, I'd like you to sit down and imagine yourself as the "new you." *Close your eyes and focus.* See yourself as you'd like to be. This is neither a trick nor a game. I assure you that, done with diligence, this will help your confidence to grow. Don't stop until you firmly *fix the image in your mind*.

14

Change Your Behavior—and Your Attitude Will Change

The importance of the *attitude* of love—of seeing beyond ourselves—was never more apparent to me than when my friend Shlomo Breznitz, a distinguished psychologist and professor at the University of Haifa in Israel, shared with me a compelling insight:

"When we study all of the research from the concentration camps," he said, "the first factor that comes up is the ability to establish meaningful relationships in the camps themselves. At first it was thought that it was the recipients who most benefited. Closer examination revealed that it was the givers who were most helped. They were able to maintain dignity and a sense of self."

He added, "The great lesson in this research is that *the best way to help oneself is to help someone else.*"

As he spoke, I was reminded of the ancient tale of the widow whose only son has died. She appeals to the holy man of her village to give her a prayer, a potion, *something* to bring back her boy. He directs her to find and to return to him a mustard seed from a home that has not known sorrow. "The mustard seed is magic," the holy man promises. "I will use it to remove the sorrow from your life."

The first house she comes to is a lavish building occupied by a wealthy family. When the family responds to her knocking, she explains her intentions—that she seeks a mustard seed from a home that has not known sorrow.

"You've come to the wrong house," the family members advise the widow, recounting the series of tragedies that had befallen them.

The widow, made sensitive by her own loss, feels great sympathy for the family and decides to stay awhile and comfort them. When she leaves, she resumes her search for the magic mustard seed. She visits the high, the low, the middle, the rich, the poor. Everywhere she goes, she finds homes with troubles—and she ministers to all she can help.

She is so busy helping others, in time she forgets her quest for the mustard seed—and she never realizes that it *was* magic: It drove the sorrow from her own life.

Do you remember your first day of school? If your first day was like mine, it was scary. Beginnings can be frightening. Suddenly the world is a *What if?* place.

What if I stumble?

What if I fail?

What if they find out I'm me?

There is, of course, something that may seem even tougher than a first experience:

Can I begin *again*?

Am I imprisoned by my past, by my failures, by my losses, by others, by the world around me?

Must I always be what I am?

Can I really be more?

Really, can I begin again?

We may choose different hairstyles, buy new clothes, reorganize our closets, paint the walls, straighten out our personal finances—but many of us resist the kind of new beginnings that can make our lives more meaningful or personally satisfying. We refuse to let go even when we know it's the right thing to do.

Why?

Change is scary.

We cling to the familiar, sometimes even when it hurts. We all know, for example, that the longer a battered spouse remains in an abusive relationship, the more difficult it is to escape. For the victim whose self-confidence has been worn away by sustained abuse, the thought of being alone, abandoned, looms larger and more terrifying with each passing day. Such fear is not limited to the abused. You may perhaps know a widow or widower of a loving spouse who cannot get beyond the grief, who refuses to face tomorrow. If you yourself have lived through a relationship that has ended, then you know it's not easy to let go.

Under *any* circumstances when we must separate from someone close to us, whether it's our choice or not, at no time do we have more need for our three allies—anxiety, fear, and anger.

We're about to explore two types of loss: when a relationship breaks up and when someone we love dies. I've introduced this section by emphasizing the anxiety of new beginnings, because that's where we're heading.

It hurts when we separate from someone we love, and we feel devastated during those first few days after a breakup. Anger and bitterness, as well as the sadness we feel, cloud insightful thinking. Said another way, our emotions overwhelm our good sense: Deep down, we know we'll *survive*, but still we ask ourselves, "Will I *prevail*?"

You will.

To see how, let's take a look at a stressful situation: Your partner is gone. Your nerves are frayed, you're sad, you hurt terribly. Maybe you're angry. . . . Okay, you're *furious*.

But here's the thing: You're also *free*. You have the opportunity for new experiences.

I don't want any.

Baloney! That was your anger talking. The truth is, regardless of the hurt and the sense of loss you feel at the moment, you are going to have new experiences. The good news is that you can choose what those experiences will be. The chance for greater joy and fulfillment is right there in front of you, waiting. The seeds of renewal are planted: *You are ready for change.*

Why?

We're most susceptible to acquiring new attitudes when we experience a change in our lives: when we graduate from high school or college, for example, or start a first job or a new job; when we retire or move; when we fall in love, establish or conclude a relationship, get married or remarried, separated or divorced; when a child is born or leaves home. When change happens—if it's important to you—you'll find your anxiety rising naturally, your adrenaline pumping. And, as with those other times when you've felt anxiety, fear, and anger, you are sharp. The world is in focus. You've never been more sensitive. So let's use this energy; let's not waste it.

When we break up with someone, it's normal to feel a loss of control, to feel helpless—especially if we're the one who has been abandoned. Our compass is spinning. We ask, "Who am I? Whom can I trust?"

Yes, that's what I feel. But how do I get back some control?

You begin by recognizing that grieving can be healthy; it can help us to absorb a loss, to place it in context. On the other hand, agonizing in self-pity and planning for revenge are not okay. If you're fixed on the past or intent on hurting someone else rather than helping yourself, you're wasting your time. And your focus is wrong:

161

Focus on solutions.

You're about to have an adventure. You have a chance for a new and better life. Your partner left—but you're still breathing. You *have* survived the breakup: "Hey, pal, I'm still standing!"

Again, remember that your goal is to regain control.

It will help to consider the words of Dr. Mimi Silbert, leader of the Delancey Street Foundation, a world-renowned treatment center for former drug abusers, prostitutes, and convicts:

"What we really mean when we say we can't do something is that we have difficulty letting go of what's comfortable. How many human beings anywhere, not just at Delancey Street, hold on to a relationship merely because it exists? This fear of loneliness, abandonment, or failure can, if we let it, hold any of us back from doing exactly what each of us needs to do to feel fulfilled."

What is taught at Delancey?

"We teach how to believe and how to love," says Mimi. "It takes unbelievable courage for the residents of Delancey. They are desperately afraid. To believe in caring and closeness—to trust—is difficult for people who have hurt others and who have been burned all their lives."

Several teaching methods and philosophies are practiced at Delancey, but one of the most effective is called *Act As If* :

A new resident at Delancey, fresh from prison, might hear: "Bill, we know you don't care about Jim over there. We know you couldn't care less whether Jim lives or dies. But, Bill, we want you to *act as if* you care about Jim."

So the new resident, to get along, pretends to care—and, to his surprise, finds that he actually does begin to care. Delancey residents transform themselves from the outside in. Against the most monumental odds—against a lifetime of rejection, failure, and disappointment—the residents of Delancey Street learn, as Mimi suggests, how to believe and how to love.

How does this apply to you?

If you change your behavior, your attitude will change.

Your attitude will change, and your confidence will grow.

CHALLENGE NO. 15:
IMAGINE A NEW YOU

In Challenge No. 11, I asked you to choose one opinion of yours that might cause discomfort for you or for someone else. Then you were to picture how differently you would behave if you did not hold that opinion. In Challenge No. 14, I asked you to focus on what you'd like to change about yourself and to imagine the "new you." Now, one more time, close your eyes, and see yourself as you'd like to be. Again, firmly fix that image in your mind. Complete this assignment before you move ahead.

Dr. Norman Vincent Peale, whose *The Power of Positive Thinking* became one of the classic inspirational books of the twentieth century, was so certain about the impact of prayer that he told me one time he was sure that we could "shoot" prayers at other people to help them. Now, *that's* power.

Your brain is hot stuff. Whether we believe it's a gift from God or the product of evolution, it is amazing: All the brain wants to do is solve problems for us.

And it's good at it.

Our problem-solving ability happens every day. Have you ever struggled with some thorny question, then given up, only to have the solution "pop" into your mind a few days later? Although you stopped consciously thinking about the problem, the computer in your brain was processing the data quietly and searching for a solution, all the while efficiently doing its other work—everything from moving your big toe and regulating your heartbeat to storing, retrieving, and analyzing words and pictures.

Along with its problem-solving capability, the human brain also can create and form images of what is not actually present—and it has the power to perceive events before they occur. If you hold an acorn in your hand, for example, can you see or feel the shade of the great oak it will become? Can you see or hear all of the life that oak will support—the insects, the birds, the squirrels? No. But you can *imagine* those results because your brain enables you to visualize what you cannot see.

To actually grow, though, we know that an acorn must take root. So we press it into the moist earth—and we wait.

To grow in confidence, to realize our dreams, to choose the life we really want, to be who we'd like to be—we need to plant some acorns, some ideas. Your brain is the fertile soil these ideas need, and it's ready. Picture your mind as two halves: One is your conscious, or thinking aloud; the other is your unconscious, or thinking silently. If we hold an image or a desire firmly and purposefully in our conscious mind, the image or desire—like a seed floating on the surface of a lake—invariably will find its way into our unconscious mind. And when our desire slips into our unconscious, action begins.

The image or desire taps into real power. There is immense energy in our unconscious—and it's pushy. Once the unconscious embraces a goal, it is determined to achieve it. The greatest actors and athletes picture their performances in detail long before they step onto a stage or enter an arena. Human beings tend to become what they imagine themselves to be: If you see yourself as confident, you become confident. If you see yourself as uncertain, you become uncertain.

Your brain is a terrific machine. It not only works to find ways in which you can be who you want to be, but, at the same time, it also encourages you to take action.

CHALLENGE NO. 16: ACT AS IF

Now you understand why, in the previous challenge, I suggested that you review Challenges No. 11 and 14 and again firmly fix the images in your mind. I wanted you to allow your brain to do its job, which is to solve problems, make plans, and look ahead. It's smart to encourage that computer in your skull to do its work—and, at the same time, tap into its power. I also hope it's apparent why I asked you earlier to stick "focus on solutions" messages all over the place. They are more than simple reminders; they are practical devices to help you drive images and desires into your unconscious mind, to keep you *thinking*.

Before we go on, we need to take a short break. What you have just read is too important for us to speed ahead. This chapter includes two of the most critical steps for a change of attitude: the one that works from the outside in, called *Act As If;* and the one that works from the inside out, called *Fix the Image in Your Mind*. Both processes are crucial to helping you solve problems, create options for yourself, build confidence, and regain control when you face either a loss or an uncertain future.

If you *act as if* you're confident, even though you may not feel sure of yourself, your confidence *will* grow. If you firmly *fix the image in your mind* of the person you'd like to be, you *will* begin to become that person.

So here's the break I'd like you to take: Please read no further for at least one day (two days, if you can stand being away from the course for that long!). Tonight and tomorrow night, before you fall off to sleep, I'd like you to imagine yourself as a professor in a classroom filled with students: You are teaching *The Confidence Course*. You plan to illustrate the processes *Act As If* and *Fix the Image in Your Mind* for your students. Make your examples as detailed and vivid as you can. And picture yourself in action. You'll have some fun with this assignment.

Enjoy.

I have suggested that grieving is a normal and necessary process and that, as long as we do not become obsessed with self-pity or seek revenge, grieving can be a healthy expression of pain: *We need to admit that we hurt.* It is a significant first step to regaining a sense of control when we suffer a disappointment, loss, or tragedy. And, as I said in Chapter 1, while we may not be able to prevent the worst from happening to us, we are responsible for our attitude toward the inevitable misfortunes that darken our lives. Bad things do happen; how we respond to them defines our character and the quality of our lives.

So, if we can't prevent disappointments, breakups, and the like, how do we regain control when loss occurs?

We exploit what we *can* control:

Although I may not be able to control the world around me, I can control me.

You control your own behavior, your own words, your own time: You determine how you will conduct yourself, what you will say and, most of the time, where you will be and for how long. You can *act as if,* and you can *fix an image in your mind.* You decide how you choose to see the world: If you change your behavior and your words, your attitude likewise will change.

How do I make these principles work in practice?
What steps should I take? How do I begin?
What I'm trying to ask is: How can I jump-start
me? How do I motivate myself to stop stalling,
get off my tail, and get moving?

You've learned two principles. Here are three steps that include both:

THREE STEPS TO CONTROLLING YOUR BEHAVIOR

1. **See your goal.**
   I mean, really see it. Be sure to imagine yourself in action. Then *fix the image in your mind*. Focus tightly. To release the power of your unconscious mind, remember that you've got to hold the desire or image firmly in your conscious mind.

2. **Sell yourself.**
   No one is more persuasive than you. If you say you cannot, you will not. You won't even start. Say, "I can." If you can see it, you can be it. Also, do not waste time looking back; do not wish for what is past or lost. Remind yourself that you're about to make a fresh start.

3. **Act as if.**
   Want to be confident? Even if you do not feel particularly confident, *act as if* you're confident.

When we experience the breakup of a meaningful relationship, as I described earlier, we are devastated. We feel lost and out of control. We have a compelling need to regain control, to direct and motivate ourselves. That's why we have to *see a goal, sell ourselves,* and *act as if* we're already there.

The truth is, despite your loss, you are going to have more experiences. So choose what you want to experience.

At every important time in your life, not only in a breakup, you have power. Even when someone dies.

Our most difficult challenge may be to recover from the death of a loved one, whether it is a friend, a parent, a spouse, or a child. This is no simple task—but it is an experience every one of us will endure and must learn to overcome. It's painful, of course, to say good-bye to someone we love. But for some people it is almost as difficult to console a survivor. That was true of me. When I was much younger, I thought funerals were barbaric. They made me very uncomfortable, and I never seemed to know what to say. It was years before I really understood that such services are a necessary catharsis for the survivors, whether it's two atheists shaking hands over the grave of a friend or the most elaborate religious ceremony.

What I had to discover was the value of a mourning period—again, the significance of grieving—and how to conduct myself comfortably and appropriately. For myself, by learning how to comfort others, I finally learned how to comfort myself at the death of someone I loved. I learned how to say good-bye. You can too.

Here's what I've come to understand:

SIX WAYS TO COMFORT THE GRIEVING

1. **Don't pretend.**
   Don't make believe you're there for some other reason. Don't divert conversation to other subjects that you consider "less painful." Survivors usually want to talk about their loss, so this should be encouraged.

2. **Don't try to make the bereaved feel better.**
   Although this may seem at first like a contradiction, it is not. I don't know how many funerals I've attended where well-meaning people have advised, "Don't take it so hard." It leaves the bereaved no response and encourages them to conceal their grief. The last time (and it was the *last* time) I said, "Don't take it so hard," a survivor asked me, "How hard should I take it?"

3. **Don't fear tears.**
   The expression of sorrow is normal, and it's better expressed than suppressed. Tears of grief are healthy tears. If stifled now, they'll erupt later—and more painfully.

4. **Do let them talk.**
   Be a good listener. The most helpful conversation may be the one in which we listen far more than we talk. Be sensitive. Again, don't discourage talk about the deceased.

5. **Do reassure.**
   When someone close to us dies, it's normal to feel guilt: Why didn't we say this or do that? How many times have we all wished: "If only I had the chance . . ." Reassure the bereaved. A kind word goes a long way here.

6. **Do call again.**
   The best friends are there the next day. There's a widely held belief that the bereaved need time to themselves. I don't think that's true. I've found

that survivors need our support more *after* all the early attention than during it.

I hope these insights help guide you when you need them. They've been invaluable to me.

Finally, if you yourself have just suffered a loss, I hope you find comfort in this thought from a note I recently sent to a friend: "As unlikely as it may seem at this moment, there will come a time when the joy of remembering is greater than the pain of loss."

CHALLENGE NO. 17: COMFORTING A FRIEND

Shlomo Breznitz said his research indicated that "the best way to help oneself is to help someone else." This principle was illustrated in the story about the widow who searched for the magic mustard seed. With this in mind, answer the following question for yourself:

How can I use this knowledge to help a friend who suffers a painful loss, whether it's the breakup of a relationship or the death of someone close?

15

How to Handle Criticism

As much as each of us might resist revealing to someone else who we really are, we must. To live our lives successfully, we need other people. We need their respect and their goodwill. When you change your hairstyle or clothes, purchase a new pair of glasses or a hat, how important to you is that first comment by another person? If you heard one hundred words of praise and one word of criticism today, which would be on your mind tonight?

Me too.

Have you ever wondered why someone else seems to handle criticism better than you do?

I have.

I can still blush today when I consider the long years of unnecessary and agonizing embarrassment I experienced before I finally understood that handling criticism is a skill we can learn; that criticism itself is an opportunity to improve ourselves and to strengthen our relationships; that criticism can be a sincere testament to friendship.

It's easier to accept criticism, I've found, when we learn not to take it personally and realize that it actually can enhance a relationship. We're most often wrong when we think: "If you criticize me, you dislike me."

Learning how to handle our emotions under criticism is a sign of maturity and is immensely valuable in the business and professional world. Socially, it's indispensable. If one spouse continually reacts to criticism with temper tantrums or other disturbing behavior, it can lead to a dangerous silence—the uneasy truce I described before. Criticism ceases, but so does communication. Eventually the marriage ends too.

The most effective way to learn how to accept criticism may be to learn how to give it. Here are six steps that have worked for me:

SIX STEPS TO GIVING CRITICISM

1. **Can it be changed?**
   If it can't, don't take the next step. Be silent.
   Never, *never* criticize what cannot be changed:
   "You shouldn't have worn that dress tonight." This kind of criticism can only hurt. If it's too late, forget it.

   This is the hardest rule to follow, because it denies us the opportunity to get it out of our system. We have to contain our disappointment with someone else when what we really want to do is tell that person off. There is enough in our lives that we can improve, however, so we ought not to waste time on what cannot be helped.

2. **Choose a proper time and place.**
    No one likes to be criticized in front of others. Also, check your mood. I'm a mean critic when I'm angry. I'll bet you are too.

3. **Reassure.**
    Begin with praise whenever possible. What good things did the person do? Be sincere. Do not say, "This is great, but . . ." Say what *is* great.

4. **Be specific.**
    If you cannot be specific, do not criticize. If you can't get it straight, how do you expect the other guy to understand?

5. **Express confidence.**
    You're criticizing something that you have already determined can be corrected. Help the person understand that he can, in fact, correct it. Then make the change seem easy to achieve.

6. **Praise improvement.**
    Be there tomorrow. To do less, after you've volunteered a criticism, is rude. If you've taken the time to criticize, take the time to praise. Not only will praise speed improvement, but further criticism from you also will likely be regarded as sincere and will be welcomed.

How can *I* best encourage someone to correct a mistake, to modify behavior, to perform more efficiently or effectively?

Pretend he's me.

What do *I* like to hear when I've flubbed?

I like my critic to reassure me that the rest of what I've done has been done well, that I'm appreciated although I slipped, that my mistake was merely human, that I wasn't lazy, irresponsible, or careless—that I can do it right, if I try again.

Once we learn how to give criticism, we can understand better how to receive it. Here is a guide:

FOUR STEPS TO TAKING CRITICISM

1. **Focus on the criticism only.**
    Do not focus on the critic, or on his emotions or your own. You and the criticism are not the same thing. Remember that a person must care about you to take the time to criticize.

2. **Find its value.**
    There may be something important that you're being told, even if the message is poorly delivered. Remember that criticism is an opportunity to improve. Ask for specifics. Be sure you understand the criticism. Don't "yes, yes" your critic. Listen to all your critic has to say. When you clearly understand the criticism, go to the next step.

3. **Evaluate.**
    If you've focused on the criticism, separated yourself from the emotion of the moment, and

clearly understood what has been suggested, then you're prepared to determine whether it is something you can change or want to change. You might ask yourself whether this is the first time you've heard this particular criticism, whether the critic is a competent (if not impartial) observer, and whether the critic is just venting frustration or actually making a valuable observation. Remember, though, a critic can vent frustration and still make a valuable observation.

4. **Say "thank you."**
   Thank the critic for his advice and enlist his help if possible.

A common fear regarding criticism is that it makes us a doormat—that accepting criticism, particularly harsh criticism, somehow demeans us. That's not necessarily true. If you exercise the steps just outlined, you—not your critic—are in control.

16

How to Take Risks

To find true security, to be confident, to know real love, to be fulfilled and to be at peace with ourselves and with others, we must learn to take risks. There's no other way. Our lives improve only when we take risks—and the first and most difficult risk we can take is to be honest with ourselves. Have you ever asked, "Do I need a change?" I have. And I've found that simply asking the question is a risk in itself. If I answer "yes," I must act—or be frustrated.

Do *you* need a change?

This chapter is meant to help you answer that question—to help you explore your opportunities and understand what happens when you actually take a risk. Then it will help you to anticipate and respond to the kind of doubts that emerge every time you reach for a goal that's larger than any you've achieved before. We will examine the dynamic factors and the three losses common to every risk. Do you want greater love, esteem, power, security? Again, *do you need a change?*

If you look up the word "risk" in your dictionary, you will find that the definition is packed with words like "danger," "hazard," "peril," "jeopardy," "exposure," "chance of injury," "damage," and "loss." Is it any wonder, then, that risk-taking makes us so anxious? After all, haven't we heard all our lives that we should avoid danger, hazards, and peril?

Clearly, taking a risk is difficult—and danger is a vital part of risk-taking. To risk is to stretch farther than we ever have before.

If taking a risk is so good for us, why do we hesitate?

Perhaps you're struggling with some of the same fears that haunted me for years. I worried that if I said what I honestly felt, for example, others would see me as I really was: *"What will I do when they find out I'm me?"* You also could be as overwhelmed as I was by what you stand to lose. Now, on top of those two common concerns, consider that most of us have been taught since childhood how not to take a risk.

As we discussed in Chapter 5, much of our own childhood involved learning what *not* to do. ("Don't touch this!" "Don't swallow that!" "Don't walk there!" "Leave that alone!") From our earliest years, we have been encouraged to respect limits. Thus, it is no surprise to find so many people believing that they are not defined by their own choices, that life happens *to* them and is not determined *by* them.

Yet risk—however much it may be discouraged when we're younger—is inescapable. Hasn't each of us faced the possibility of a new job, a move, the gain or loss of friends or lovers? Hasn't each of us, particularly as we've grown older, avoided some opportunity because we resisted being seen as a beginner, an amateur?

And when we're really honest with ourselves, what is it we are most afraid of?

> ***I don't want to fail, and I don't want
> to be embarrassed.***

Yes. The fear of failure and humiliation rises in any normal human being faced with important choices.

> ***Okay, I'm normal—but can I actually learn to
> reduce the nervousness I feel when facing risks?***

Yes, you can. Let's begin now.

CHALLENGE NO. 18: GOALS

I'd like you to focus on two questions that almost all students ask while taking *The Confidence Course*: *What do I really want? What do I need?* You've worked hard to get to this point. You've had to reassess your attitudes, swap perceptions, challenge yourself. You've had to write a lot—and *think*. I know that these lessons and challenges are no picnic in the park. But, as I'm sure you've come to recognize, these exercises help build confidence. Yes, this stuff works. So let's get to it.

Before you read further, weigh again those two questions: *What do I really want? What do I need?* If you can, state the answers as "goals." We're now going to explore the risks we'll have to take to achieve these goals. Again, please write down your answers. And remember that goals change. You do not have to feel that you're carving your future in marble. Breathe easily and take your time.

The essence of every risk may be found in a single question: "What is it that I want but am afraid to reach for?" From our first breath, we desire more. And whatever we seek—be it love, power, self-esteem—what stands in our way?

I believe it is *fear of losses.*

When we face a risk, isn't our chief concern what we may lose? Yet, ironically, more often than not we fail to identify clearly what those losses might be. Sometimes all we have is a queasy feeling that we're going to lose *something.* By itself, that shadowy suspicion has stopped me in my tracks more than once. When I can't identify my losses, my anxiety blossoms. I've found that at the very moment when the pressure to take a risk is greatest, I feel the strongest urge to retreat.

Fortunately, I've learned that to take risks intelligently, I must appreciate three losses contained in every worthwhile risk:

THE THREE RISKS

1. The positive loss.
2. The practical loss.
3. The potential loss.

The positive loss is a loss of innocence or ignorance. This happens when I admit to myself that I am no longer content in a situation. Such an admission makes me uncomfortable because, once I've admitted the truth, I have to make a choice: Do nothing and continue to be dissatisfied or take a chance and risk the consequences. Contentment is gone. When a worker says, "I don't like my job," he or she accepts a positive loss. When a woman declares, "My boyfriend is a deadbeat," she accepts a positive loss. When a student decides, "I need more education," he or she accepts a positive loss.

The practical loss, the second loss contained in every worthwhile risk, is what I have to leave behind in order to move forward. To take a new job, for example, I must give up the old. Similarly, to enjoy a new romance, the woman will have to lose that deadbeat boyfriend. And to live away at college, a student must leave home. Although a positive loss means we have to make a choice, most of the anxiety we feel is because of our practical loss. Like soldiers at war, most of us will struggle far more strenuously to hold on to what we have than to gain something new. It is not easy to let go—even when it's a job we hate or a relationship that saddens us.

The potential loss is the tangible loss that may occur if I take a risk and it does not work out as I had hoped. The potential loss is usually the easiest to identify, and it is the one that is most discussed: What if I get fired from the new job? What if my new romance sours? What if I fail at college?

CHALLENGE NO. 19: ACCEPTING LOSS

Review your answers to the questions "What do I really want?" and "What do I need?" It is perfectly healthy for you to desire more for yourself. That's one of the best parts of being a human being: *We are meant to grow.* And keep in mind that the essence of every risk is contained in the question "What is it that I want but am afraid to reach for?"

I've taken risks and failed. Yet I know that the only risks I regret are the ones I didn't take. The times that I've gone no further than accepting a positive loss—recognizing that I was not happy but refusing to take a risk—have been more painful to me than any failure. Why? Because I'm left to wonder, "*What if* I had taken the chance?" I will never know. Conversely, I have learned something from every risk I've taken, however it has turned out.

It's normal to be afraid of consequences when facing risk. Your assignment is to identify your positive, practical, and potential losses. Write them down. Then answer this question: "Which losses will be the most difficult for me to accept?"

How have you learned to measure your life?

In the United States we insist that children start kindergarten at a particular time in their lives, and we expect them to graduate from high school in their middle to late teens. Our companies, when not prevented by labor laws from insisting upon mandatory retirement, create programs to encourage those of a particular age—often as young as fifty-five—to leave. Why? We expect (and frequently we require) that people at certain ages behave as we think they should. How old must a person be to purchase liquor? So many times we hear, *"Act your age."* It's told to the ten-year-old girl who paints her face with gooey globs of makeup, slips on her mother's high heels, and lights a Marlboro. And the same advice is given to the grandfather as he mounts his Harley Davidson motorcycle, picks up his much younger girlfriend, and scoots off to a nightspot. We've learned to gauge our lives, our progress—often our value as human beings—by our age, and no measure known to humankind has been more imprecise.

I believe that we are constantly encouraged to internalize a calendar that causes undue distress, disappointment, and even tragedy.

What is the "right" age? Sometimes it seems to me that we're given a report card, and our grades are dependent on a point in time: I married "late"; I married "early." How often do we ask, "Am I doing okay for my age?" "Am I too young?" "Am I too old?" This, in a century when life expectancy continually increases. When is "middle age"? Forty, sixty, seventy-five?

Chronological age is a flimsy guide to our health, to our career status, to most of our real needs. How emotionally secure is the twenty-nine-year-old who has taken risk upon risk to become a vice president but who is now depressed because she won't be president by thirty? How adult is the widower who first risks marrying a younger woman, then refuses to risk having the child they both want because he worries about how it will look?

My point is not to deny that the timing of crucial events in our lives is important. Quite the contrary. If your mother dies when you're seven, undoubtedly the impact is greater than if she dies when you're thirty-seven.

Risk is often thrust upon us when we least expect it— and how we respond to it determines the quality of our lives.

I've found that the most successful risk-takers prevail over unexpected challenges by the strength of their convictions. What distinguishes the most accomplished people on earth is not some inner peace but rather how they've learned to organize their lives around an idea and to focus on it, despite turmoil. They are adult: They see beyond themselves.

As you and I should.

I stated before that the challenges worth taking are those that lead to the most fulfilling life: When we commit to high ideals, we succeed before the outcome is known. That truth, you may recall, was the basis of the second of the Seven Steps to Self-Fulfillment, which is to *believe in something big*. I also said that it's not possible for either you or me to be an empty bucket. Human beings are not made that way. *Everyone believes in something.* It might be God or no God. It could be greed for money or power, a career or a friend, science, a principle . . . *something.* Whatever it is we place before ourselves—whatever it is we believe—is what we run toward. A story told to me by Father Joseph Kelly of St. Anthony's Church in the Bronx, New York, might be useful. It's about a young priest who began to doubt his vocation:

One afternoon, as he walked down a city street in the dead of winter, the young priest passed a small boy—homeless, skinny, his jacket threadbare, his tiny body huddled over a street grate as he tried to absorb the heat from the subway tunnel below.

"God!" the priest exclaimed, his frustration at a boil.

He looked back at the shivering child.

"God," he demanded, "why do you allow this? Why don't you do something about it? Don't you give a damn?"

In his mind, to his astonishment, he heard for the first time what he knew was the voice of his Lord:

"I *do* care," he was told, "and I *have* done something about it. I created *you.*"

CHALLENGE NO. 20: RISKS

Let's take another look at the needs you described in the last two exercises. When you redefined them as goals and risks, you probably discovered that your practical losses would be the most difficult to take.

They usually are. It's always hard to give up what we have and what we know. To build your self-confidence and create a better life for yourself, however, you simply have to let go: *You must take chances.*

If you do nothing, you reduce the possibilities you have for greater joy. When we avoid taking risks, inevitably we have to settle for less.

So, what I'd like you to do now is take one more step toward taking a risk. As candidly as possible (remember, no one else is going to see what you write down), weigh whether your needs and goals involve mainly "trust," "identity," or "larger purpose."

One student, for example, told me her greatest desire was to be famous. Thus, "identity" was key. If her goal had been to help others, then I might have called it "larger purpose." If she had said, "I want to be respected," then both "identity" and "larger purpose" might be involved. If she had declared, "I want friends," we could probably include all three elements, with one more important than the others. What do you think?

If your risk is specific ("I want to be promoted to the position of assistant supervisor in my department"), then describe what it is that you're afraid of. When you do that, I'm sure you'll discover elements of *trust, identity,* or *larger purpose.*

WHEN RISK IS A MATTER OF LIFE OR DEATH

In the thirty years since I served in Vietnam, I have noticed many people who speak easily in the language of combat even though they have never worn a military uniform. It can be unnerving. I've heard business leaders pledge to "wage battles" in the marketplace, to "take no prisoners," to "seek out and destroy" competitors. I've been astounded when ambitious executives described a corporate challenge with the words: "This is war."

No, it is not. *War* is war.

Thus, you can understand why I decided one day to ask a real warrior about risk. I needed to speak with someone who really does make life-or-death choices—a leader who has to decide who in his unit will face an enemy in mortal combat. Not the game, the event.

I asked the commandant of the United States Marine Corps, General Charles C. Krulak, what he thought his men gained from the special emphasis on taking risks that the Marine Corps, in particular, places on its troops from the very first days of basic training.

"Testing ourselves against the unknown," he told me, "proving to ourselves what we can do, building our confidence by facing uncertainty and prevailing—these are the actions that build self-confidence, esprit, and cohesion under pressure. *Taking a risk is necessary both to grow and to develop a pattern of success.* For Marines as individuals and for the corps as a whole, learning how to handle risk is fundamental to our success in combat.

"Risk is inherent in combat and in responding to situations that may lead to combat. The battlefield is filled with uncertainty. To function effectively, Marines must be able to act intelligently in the face of uncertainty.

"By taking a calculated risk, by taking well-conceived action despite not having all the information we would like to have, we are able to exploit opportunities: *On the battlefield, we can never know everything we want to about an enemy—but neither can we wait for a perfect situation.* Every mission involves risk. You cannot take an objective, rescue a downed pilot, evacuate an embassy, without taking risks."

And neither you nor I can achieve our goals, fulfill our needs, without taking risks.

17

How to Find Courage

You have been encouraged to search through your experience for hidden obstacles that could hold you back. To change your life, though, you must do more than calculate the possible consequences of a risk. You must act.

So, let's move forward.

When I have had to make crucial choices in my life, I have been helped by the advice that the actress Marlo Thomas gave me years ago. I had asked her what she thought stood in the way of anyone achieving a dream: "When we line up all the facts that we believe are against us," she told me, "the facts can stop us before we start. Whatever we need to discourage us we can uncover: 'I'm too young, too old, too short, too tall, unprepared, inexperienced, or not quite ready.' And if we miss a few details, we can always find someone to help us 'face the facts.' The facts, after all, speak for themselves—except they're not true. All the facts together mean nothing. What matters more is what you really want, what you're willing to work for, to struggle for, to take risks for."

As Marlo advised, you need to know not only what is at risk but also why. Pursue your own dreams—not your mother's, your lover's, or your friend's. Be sure that your choices are indeed *your* choices. When we decide who we are (*what I am, what I have, what I seem to be*) and when we frankly reveal to ourselves *why* we're facing a risk, we're learning how to be adults.

Risks would inspire far less worry if they followed a pattern, with each question leading predictably to the next, more difficult question. But risks are not rungs on a ladder. A risk is like an ever-widening gap across an opening drawbridge. We don't step; we *leap* across a risk. That's why risks inspire fear: How can we know what our boss will say about our resignation until we hand it to him? Neither can we know how a lover will respond until we actually risk saying good-bye. Risks are scary precisely because there is an unknown.

If we could predict with complete accuracy what would occur if we took a risk, we would feel no anxiety. We worry only because we care. We don't fret about what's meaningless to us. Thus, with fear in mind, we come to another factor in risk-taking: courage.

Courage, as I've said, is always and only one thing: It is acting with fear, not without it:

To be brave, we must be afraid.

The television talk-show host Denise Richardson described to me one day how she had learned to bungee-jump. Perched on a bridge platform twenty-two stories above the water, she understandably was frightened. Her instructor told her to consider what she felt at the moment. It was, as you may suspect, very unpleasant. He said that as long as she clung tightly to the bridge, she would continue to feel the agonizing sting of fear; but if she jumped, she'd feel exhilaration. "Up here is pain," he said. "Down there is joy. Which would you rather feel?"

Denise leaped. And she told me later, "He was right."

Risk-taking builds confidence. The more risks we take, the better we get at it. You can learn to master the process of risk-taking without leaping from a bridge. Most important, you can find within yourself the noble motives to realize your dreams.

Have you heard the ancient fable of the little eagle that would not take a good look at itself?

Quite by accident, a farmer found an eagle's egg on a hill. He carried it to the chicken coop near his barn and plopped it alongside some eggs in the nest of a hen. Later, the eagle hatched among a brood of chicks.

As the eagle grew, it did what chickens do, since it was convinced that it was a chicken: It clucked. It flapped its wings to fly a few feet in the air. Like the real chickens, it searched for no more exotic food than the seeds and insects it found by scratching the earth.

One day the eagle looked up into the sky and saw the most dazzling creature it had ever seen.

"What is that?" it asked, startled by the sheer majesty of the form soaring gracefully in wide circles in and out of the high clouds.

"That," a rooster said in a hushed, reverent tone, "is an eagle, the greatest of all birds."

"Wow, I'd like to do that!"

"Forget it," the rooster advised. "We're different."

So the little eagle forgot—and when it died a year later, it died believing it was a chicken.

Do you recognize the little eagle? Sometimes that's us, isn't it?

Fortunately, we have the personal power, if we tap into it, to soar from our nests. We can examine our own experiences and grow. We can worry well, which is to direct our anxiety and our anger into positive channels. We can focus on solutions. When it seems safer to cluck, remember that you were made to soar. You have moved yourself in that direction, made an act of trust, by working at *The Confidence Course*.

Now that we know how to find the courage to soar, we're ready to review the Seven Steps to Taking Risks:

SEVEN STEPS TO TAKING RISKS

1. **Assume responsibility.**
   Your life is yours alone—and to live it as an adult is to accept that no single risk can solve all of your problems, achieve all of your dreams, or even be

enough. To want to be more than we are is real and normal and healthy.

2. **Define a clear goal.**
   We cannot succeed if we stumble here. Without a clear goal, we cannot know our progress in a risk—or even be sure when to quit. (When I asked the entertainer Carol Burnett what she was most afraid of, she replied: "To wake up one morning and discover that I have no goal. *That* would be frightening.")

3. **Review your positive, practical, and potential losses.**
   The truth is, it is difficult to accept a loss, particularly a practical loss. When you have to decide to let go, though, you may find useful the advice that Denise Richardson heard from her bungee instructor high atop the bridge: "Up here is pain," he said. "Down there is joy. Which would you rather feel?"

4. **Ask, "Am I responding as a child, as an adolescent, or as an adult?"**
   Is the risk itself mainly about trust, about getting a better sense of your own identity or about something even larger? I've learned from experience that when we focus on risks that have a larger purpose, we can't go wrong. Even if the risk doesn't turn out as we hoped it would, we will gain from it. But beware: Risks taken because we're hurt or angry or jealous are usually unwise and unrewarding, whatever their outcome.

5. **Decide.**

   But before you do, let's consider some advice from Hugh Downs, a fellow who has taken many risks— from conquering his fear of water to being cohost of *20/20*: "If we start by taking small risks first," he advises, "we're encouraged to take larger risks. And if we know clearly what's at stake, we can take risks more wisely. For example, if I was asked whether I'd drive a car at one hundred and twenty-five miles per hour on Route 101, I'd have to reply, 'Yes and no.' Just to drive it, I'd say, 'No.' The risk is too great. However, if I was told that my child was down the highway, in serious trouble, and urgently needed my help, I'd say, 'Yes.' And, of course, to give ourselves the best chance for success with any risk, we must prepare well. . . . I must prepare as if my life depends on it—because, after all, it does."

6. **Check your timing.**

   But don't use that legitimate concern as an excuse to hesitate. In every critical risk, there is, of course, a moment too soon—a point at which we're not ready, either emotionally or substantially, to go forward. If we try, we fail. But timing is rarely perfect for any risk. Life is too unpredictable. Thus, the best—and the smartest—we can be is honest: "When is the best time to take the risk? What will happen if I don't act *then*?" Certainly, if we're as impulsive as we can be as adolescents, we increase our likelihood of failure. But, more often than not, our concern over whether it's too soon to take a risk is really an excuse to dawdle, to further rationalize why not to act. *You* know where you are. It *is* time.

And now that you've climbed six of the steps, you're ready to take that risk.

7. **Act.**
   You *can* be confident. You've earned it.

Number six of the Seven Steps to Self-Fulfillment is essential to what you've learned about risk-taking:

THE SIXTH STEP TO SELF-FULFILLMENT

1. Know who is responsible.
   Accept personal responsibility for your behavior.
   When you say, "I am responsible," you can build a new life, even a new world.
2. Believe in something big.
   Your life is worth a noble motive.
3. Practice tolerance.
   You will like yourself a lot more, and so will others.
4. Be brave.
   Remember, courage is acting *with* fear,

not without it. If the challenge is important to you, you're supposed to be nervous.

5. Love someone.
Because you should know joy.

6. **Be ambitious.**
No single effort will solve all of your problems, achieve all of your dreams, or even be enough. To want to be more than we are is real and normal and healthy.

Again, no single effort will solve all your problems, achieve all your dreams, or even be enough. To want to be more than we are is real and normal and healthy.

18

How to Give a Great Talk

You have been asked to speak before a group. Are fuzzy butterflies dancing in your belly? Will you be talking to an audience of three friends, three hundred colleagues, or three thousand strangers? No matter. Knees shake regardless of room size. Of course, there is a question that tends to pop up at a time like this: "What do I do now?"

Cheers! I have good news for you. You are going to give a great talk. And, as unlikely as it may seem at the moment, you probably will enjoy the experience. Why? Because you are going to learn four simple steps to an effective presentation:

Four Elements of Effective Talks
1. **Research what you're going to say.**
2. **Organize what you're going to say.**

3. **Rehearse what you're going to say.**
4. **Say it.**

1. RESEARCH

We begin with homework. A great talk starts here, with three distinct tasks:

First, answer the question, "What is my message?" You're going to sell *something*. What is it?

Second, list in order of importance the key points that you need to make. Gather appropriate facts, statistics, and stories that support each key point.

Third, answer the question, "After I finish my great talk, what do I expect from my audience?" You must know *why* and *to whom* you'll be speaking. (Among other questions, whenever I'm invited to speak, I always ask: "Who are the people who will be in the audience? What do you want my talk to accomplish? How will I know if I succeeded?")

You can be sure that we all listen to the same radio station, WIIFM—*What's In It For Me?* With this in mind, be sure you include in your research a sentence that describes what need your message will fill for the audience.

Do *you* believe your message? You can stumble and fumble over words, say the wrong thing, forget where you are, trip as you walk to the podium. (I've done all of these things.) But if you are sincere—if you believe what you're saying—the audience will eagerly give you a second, a third, even a fourth chance. Why? Audiences want to be won over.

However, if you are insincere, if you do not believe what you are going to say—no matter how well you technically handle all else—you almost certainly will fail. Don't be a phony. Be smart: Choose a message that you are genuinely enthusiastic about. And there should be a catchy title somewhere in the sentence that announces your message.

2. ORGANIZE

If you've prepared your research thoroughly, you've collected more than you need. Good! Let's edit. You already have listed key points. Well, which do you really need? Write each as a simple sentence. Next, choose three facts (fewer, if possible) to support those key points. Now, if the fate of the earth depended upon your choosing only one fact to support each point, which would it be? State each fact as a simple sentence and place it alongside its proper key point.

Moving right along (I love editing!), what one story best illustrates your entire message?

Let's take a look at where you are now:

- **You sincerely believe what you're going to say.**
- **You have a catchy title right there in the message sentence.**
- **You have key points, with each supported by singularly strong evidence.**
- **You have a relevant story that ties it all together.**

It looks to me like you have the makings of a great talk. Let's go.

3. Rehearse.

You will be using only the bare-bones outline you've just created for your first rehearsal:

- **Title**
- **Key points**
- **Evidence**
- **Story**

Before we go further, though, let's check on your story. It should follow the first two fundamental rules for storytelling, which we learned in Chapter 9:

1. **Pick a story for your audience.**
2. **Pick a story you like.**

Again, whether you have an audience of one or an audience of one hundred million, the two rules apply.

Okay, you're ready.

4. Say it.

Everything you need at this point won't even fill a single sheet of paper: You have an idea, an outline, a few sentences. With this material alone, find a quiet spot, set your watch so that you can time yourself, turn on a tape recorder, and give your talk.

Whoa! Where do I begin?

As the late Alex Haley said about storytelling, "Start at the beginning and tell the earliest thing that happened." Tell your story first. Imagine, for example, that your goal is to inspire a class of students to continue their education, and you choose the following true story to illustrate your message:

THE DUMMY

The little boy lived in Detroit with his brother and his mother, who had married at thirteen but had since divorced. His name was Ben, but the other kids in his fifth-grade class called him "The Dummy."

Deeply worried, their mother ordered Ben and his brother to write two book reports for her to read every week. Thus, they began regular visits to the Detroit Public Library.

One day, Ben's science teacher held up a shiny, black rock and asked the class if anyone knew what it was. No one responded. Ben raised his hand. He would remember the moment all his life: "Everyone turned around and looked, and they started poking at each other and laughing because they knew I was going to say something really stupid."

But, amid the titters, Ben stood, correctly identified the rock, and told the class how it had been formed. His fellow students were flabbergasted. And Ben liked what he felt: "It was at that moment," he'd recall later, "that I realized I wasn't stupid." He knew the answer because he had been reading books. So he asked himself, "Aren't I tired of being a dummy? What if I read books in all of my subjects?"

By the middle of the sixth grade, Ben had risen to the top of his class. He did well again in high school, then attended and was graduated from both Yale University and the University of Michigan Medical School.

At age thirty-three, he was named director of pediatric neurosurgery at Johns Hopkins Hospital in Baltimore. And it was he, Dr. Benjamin Carson, who in 1987 led the team that performed the world's first successful separation of Siamese twins joined at the back of the head. He also pioneered a number of other surgical procedures.

By the way, what young Ben did not know was that his mother—because of her limited third-grade education—was not able to read those book reports that she had assigned to her two sons.

Did you enjoy this true story? If it moved *you*, it will move your audience.

Okay, you have begun with a story. Now give your key points. Speak slowly. Cite your evidence. *Speak slowly.* Conclude by referring back to your Ben Carson story, perhaps with words like these:

"Now, who among you wants to be like Ben Carson?

(Pause)

"He would be the first to say you can. You *can* live your dreams . . . *if* you do what Dr. Carson did:

"Value learning. Take advantage of school. Do the smart thing.

"*I* know you can. I hope *you* do too.

(Pause)

"Thank you."

The students may not remember all of your key points

or other evidence, but it is likely that they won't soon forget the little boy called "The Dummy." That's power—and you have it within your grasp. *You* are a storyteller. As I reminded you in Chapters 8 and 9, you have been hearing and telling stories all of your life. Storytelling is so much a part of our lives that we may take it for granted and fail to recognize its power over us and everyone else. Truly, a well-told story can amuse, disarm, teach, and motivate; it can make a point, win a friend, or close a sale.

Again, follow the two firm rules in choosing a story: Pick a story for your audience. Pick a story you like.

Then tell your wonderful story as simply—and briefly—as you can. Complex stories are hard to tell and even harder to follow. (I could have described Ben Carson's admirable family life today or the many important honors he has received. Actually, whole books have been devoted to this man's achievements.) *Keep it simple*.

And let your stories sell themselves. Never say things like, "This is a really funny story" or, "Wait till you hear how this one ends!" Just tell your story—and be sure that everything you say leads to the story's conclusion. Don't take side streets; they are tedious. (Remember what I did not tell you about Ben Carson.) Finally, you should know how *tension* is created and *discovery* is made in every story you share. As explained in Chapter 8, tension and discovery are what rivet an audience, hold its attention, and make a story absorbing.

We find that tension occurs in real life because none of us knows for sure what's going to happen next. Tension is what makes life interesting. We're curious; we anticipate. Tension in life is authentic. A well-told story is similar—except that the tension of a story is artificially created. Storytellers build tension by asking or implying a question as early in a tale as possible. Whenever that question is answered—when the discovery is made—the tension ends.

Consider some of the questions raised early in the Ben Carson story: Who is Ben? Will he always be "The Dummy"? Will the book reports help him? Will he raise his hand in the classroom? Will he answer the question correctly? Will he be humiliated? There's a universal question in the Ben Carson story that touches each of us: *What will I do when they find out I'm me?* The greatest risk we can take is to allow others to see us as we really are: When Ben stood, we all stood. The large question is, will Ben prevail? That's why the story can continue until we find out (discovery) who Ben is today and we're touched by the truth (second discovery) that Ben's mother could not read.

You can be confident in a story that has tension.

So, with a good story under your belt, a title, key points, and evidence at hand, you are ready to start rehearsing again.

Go back to that quiet spot of yours, start your recorder, check your watch—and *talk*.

As soon as you finish, play back the recording. (Like most people, I cringe at the sound of my own voice on tape. If you do too, that's okay. Listen anyway.)

Rehearse again, this time with more feeling.

Picture yourself in front of your audience. You desperately want them to understand.

Can you see their eyes? *See their eyes.*

Don't let your sentences trail off. That's a common weakness in far too many speakers. *Speak clearly* to the very end of your sentences.

How is your posture? Don't slouch.

Rehearse again—but this time in front of a mirror.

Act as if this is the real thing. Don't pick up bad habits; they are hard to correct. All of the great dancers, singers, and actors are as conscientious in practice as they are when they go onstage. That's why they are who they are. They don't get that good in performance; they get that good in rehearsal. The best performers know that every move counts. If you're lax here, you'll be lax there.

When I was rehearsing to perform *Talkin' Stuff* in Washington, D.C., in 1992, Carol Burnett gave me sage advice: "Know your script like the back of your hand. If you were pulled from a deep sleep and someone gave you a line, you should be able to respond immediately with the next line. That will help you to control your anxiety. And, even more important, *if you know your script well, you'll be able to leave it.*"

Leave the script?

Yes!

The whole point is communication. You are never at a podium to *talk*; you are there to *persuade*. If you do not know your talk well enough to amend it, as Carol prepared me to do, you give up one of the most important tools you have: your ability to observe and respond.

Ask yourself: "When I speak with someone, don't I pay attention to how that person responds?" I'll bet you watch the other person carefully. If someone turns away from you or averts his eyes when you speak, for example, you probably talk faster or slower, speak with greater emphasis or stop talking. Every day, we adjust our behavior to other people's responses. It's the same onstage or at a microphone. Why?

People sit as a group, but they hear you individually.

A performance or a talk is *personal.* Whether your audience is eight colleagues at a conference table, eight hundred strangers in a stadium, or eight million viewers watching you on their televisions, you entertain one person at a time.

So, let's take another look at your talk. Can we slice off some fat or add some muscle? To trim weight, can your facts be stated more clearly, more vividly, or (I am always an editor) in fewer words? To add strength, do you have some colorful anecdotes or humor that can help illustrate your key points?

Good. Let's move along.

Put your notes aside. Do not refer to them. Believe me, you can do this, and the results will be well worth your effort. With your watch set and your tape recorder turned on, stand before a mirror, make eye contact with yourself, and talk once more.

How was your time? Are you speaking clearly to the end of each sentence? Good posture?

We're going to do something a little different now. Sit in a soft chair or on a couch. Take some deep breaths. Now relax through your body parts. Starting at your toes, feel yourself loosen up: your feet, your legs, into your chest. Let your fingers relax, then your hands, wrists, arms, shoulders, and neck.

When you are relaxed, close your eyes and imagine yourself at the podium, giving a dynamic talk. See yourself in action: You are confident. You speak clearly to the end of your sentences. Your gestures are natural. You make eye contact. You are enthusiastic. You enjoy what you're doing. You are smiling.

Do this for fifteen to twenty minutes (longer if you'd like).

When you're ready, return to your quiet spot with your watch and tape recorder—and talk.

That rehearsal accomplished, put everything away. Have some fun: a movie, television, a party, a book. Get a good night's sleep. You've earned it.

Starting the next day, practice your story with listeners who are not aware that you are rehearsing. Slip in key points when you can. Observe how they respond as you speak, but do *not* ask for approval. ("So, Sam, did you like that story?")

We're almost there.

Continue to practice the relaxation exercise every day and envision yourself distinctly, speaking confidently. Rehearse your talk as often as you can alone—and again in front of as many different people as you can find. (A student in *The Confidence Course* once asked me if "over-rehearsing" is a concern. "No," I explained, "because, if you truly believe in something—be it a story or a whole talk—you will tell it every time with enthusiasm. Did you ever hear a sports fan go on about his favorite team?")

There's a good chance you will find yourself actually looking forward to speaking. Before you reach for that microphone, though, I'd like to share some valuable lessons I've learned about audiences:

FIVE SECRETS ABOUT AUDIENCES

1. **People in an audience will care about you—if you care about them.**

   Don't *tell* an audience that you care; *show* that you care. Share your enthusiasm: Allow your audience to feel your passion.

   Make eye contact with as many people as you can. *Include everybody.* Don't perform "termite theater." That's what happens when speakers fix their gaze on the podium or the floor; they're talking to the termites. *Look up.* When we speak with people in small groups, we naturally include all of those present. To do otherwise is rude. We should treat our audiences with the same respect.

   I mentally divide a room into sections, find one person in each section to lock eyes with, then return to him or her throughout the talk. Many of the folks seated around that person will be sure that I'm looking directly into their eyes. If the room is darkened, I picture people's faces in my mind, and I act as if I can see them.

   Always *embrace your audience.* And, most

important, when you prepare well (which is why you rehearse), an audience knows you care. It shows.

2. **Every effective talk is a dialogue between a speaker and an audience.**
Be listener-oriented. Remember, they are hearing you one at a time. Performers who "watch themselves" will fall flat. Such people are self-absorbed, and everyone knows it. Listen to your audience, not to yourself.

3. **When we focus on our audience, we reduce our anxiety.**
And when we pay attention to an audience's responses and we know our lines well, as Carol Burnett advised, we can diverge from our script with real confidence.

Let's say, for example, that you foul up. But you laugh at yourself—which is probably how you would respond among a group of friends. Most likely, the audience will laugh *with* you. The slip was unexpected. If you know your talk well, you can do more than handle a flub: You can touch your audience.

Audiences want to laugh: Lines that may not seem that funny among two or three people sometimes will make a larger audience howl.

Another example of proper focus would be an instance in which you can feel how moved your audience was by a story you just told or a point you made, so you comment on their response: "Thank

you. I guess you can tell that it touches me too."
That's genuine—and it's appreciated.

The key is the sincerity of your desire to
communicate. Do you believe what you're saying?
Is it important to you to communicate your
message? Audiences cherish enthusiasm, and they
understand nervousness.

4. **Audiences love to discover.**
    "I'm going to prove to you the importance of
    education. I'll begin by telling you a story. . . ."
    Well, that's one way to introduce Dr. Carson, the
    neurosurgeon. Here's another: "I'd like to share a
    story. It's about a little boy named Ben. . . ."
    Choose the second opening, and you can be
    confident that the audience will understand the
    story's meaning. Then, if you'd like, add at the
    end: "Education is important, isn't it?" Your
    audience will agree: *Audiences are smart.*

    Sometimes, of course, the only way to open is to
    state your message first. Opening with a joke is a
    similar device. It's okay, but it is a crutch—
    probably one you won't need.

    Why?

    A well-told story is the sharpest tool you'll ever
    wield.

5. **If I read, you'll sleep; if I *talk*, you'll listen.**
    Unless it is out of your control and you absolutely
    must, do not *read* a talk: *Talk* your talk. If you
    must read—because the nation demands it, the
    Constitution requires it, or the corporation

insists—then you must know your talk so well that your eyes can leave the printed page and find human beings to lock in with. And remember these three rules: pause, pause, pause.

If you're convinced that you need notes, here's something you can do: On a single sheet, list your key points in order. (Since you know you're going to begin with your wonderful story and refer back to it when you conclude, you don't have to write it all down.) Keep the sheet on your person. If you must, place it on the podium.

If you plan to use any props, charts, or illustrations, do not talk to them. When you speak, *look at your audience.* Don't place anything between you and your listeners.

Now there's only one thing left to do:

Relax.

You are not going to die—and you will not be swallowed up by the earth. In fact, you'll find that the more you speak, the more confident you become. Further, your *desire* to speak will increase. And you will be able to vary and build on what you've learned here. When you feel an audience's sincere appreciation for your effort, you will be exhilarated—and that's habit-forming.

The anxiety every sane person feels before a talk is not only normal and healthy, it is invaluable. Anxiety is your ally. It reaches its peak just before you speak (what Jerry Lewis calls his "fifteen-second moment," when his hands grow moist, he fumbles with his bow tie, and he paces—still, after more than half a century of performing). Without anxiety, a great talk cannot occur. It is simply not possible.

A great talk requires the energy that only anxiety provides.

So, take deep breaths. Relax, just as you did when you were rehearsing.

You are ready.

19

How to Choose the Life You Want

Why did you take *The Confidence Course*?

Perhaps you made the decision because you wanted to strengthen your resolve or reduce your anxieties and fears. Or maybe you just wanted to be better able to answer for yourself: *Who am I? What do I want to do?*

This chapter concludes your search with a review. It is concise, but I think you'll agree that its message is substantial. Let's start with a quick look back.

I promised in the very first chapter that I would show you how to make yourself more confident:

The Confidence Course, anchored in practical life experience, will work for you because we can transform ourselves. The truth is, you and I define who we are every day by the choices we make, and thus we choose who we want to be. I create myself. So do you. I invent myself. You do too. You and I are not what we eat; we are what we *think*. Confidence, by definition, is an attitude—and your attitude toward people and situations, just like mine, is subject to change. You're going to learn here how to swap one set of perceptions for another. The world will remain the same; how you *see* the world will be different.

This chapter completes the circle with the last of the Seven Steps to Self-Fulfillment:

THE SEVENTH STEP TO SELF-FULFILLMENT

1. Know who is responsible.

    Accept personal responsibility for your behavior. When you say, "I am responsible," you can build a new life, even a new world.

2. Believe in something big.

    Your life is worth a noble motive.

3. Practice tolerance.

    You will like yourself a lot more, and so will others.

4. Be brave.

    Remember, courage is acting *with* fear, not without it. If the challenge is important to you, you're supposed to be nervous.

5. Love someone.

    Because you should know joy.

6. Be ambitious.

    No single effort will solve all of your problems, achieve all of your dreams, or even be enough. To want to be more than we are is real and normal and healthy.

7. **Smile.**

   Because no one else can do this for you.

This rule, like the very first, reminds us to accept personal responsibility for our lives—and it also suggests a choice each of us has to make.

CHALLENGE NO. 21:
THE CHOICES WE MAKE

On the left side of a single sheet of paper, write in a column three words: "Appearance," "Language," and "Behavior." On the right side, write in a column three words: "People," "Information," and "Places." At the bottom of the page, across the middle, write "Time." Pick up the sheet of paper.

Appearance	People
Language	Information
Behavior	Places

Time

You hold in your hand the potential of your life on this planet. The words describe seven choices you make every day that determine the nature and quality of your experience.

217

Picture yourself in a house with two doors, one marked "out," the other marked "in." The words on the left are what you send out; the words on the right are what you allow in.

SEVEN CHOICES WE MAKE DAILY

1. **Appearance.**

   You select the clothes you wear; the soaps, cosmetics, and fragrances you use; the length and style of your hair; how clean and healthy-looking you choose to be.

2. **Language.**

   You pick your own words, finish your own sentences, and express yourself in gestures.

3. **Behavior.**

   You decide how you respond to people and circumstances.

   Appearance, language, and behavior are the decisions you make that allow the world to know you: You paint the portrait others see. You determine how you look, what you say, how you act.

   And, every day, the world outside paints a portrait of itself for you. It has three features:

4. **People.**

   Whom do you choose to talk with? Whom do you allow to give you advice, comfort, friendship? Whom do you encourage to be part of your life?

   Whom do you allow in?

5. **Information.**

Which messages do you choose to receive? Most of us live in a blizzard of words, sounds, and pictures: television, radio, movies, computers, discs, tapes, books, newspapers, magazines, pamphlets, lectures, sermons, conversations.

What do you allow in?

6. **Places.**

How do the places where you spend most of your time affect the quality of your life? Do they help you to feel fulfilled?

Why do you choose to be in these places?

While the world outside strives mightily to influence us, it is we ourselves who choose *who, what,* and *why.* And we also choose *when:*

7. **Time.**

"Time"—the word across the bottom of your page—is under your control. You choose when to take action.

To reach the end of this course you've had to make many choices. And I congratulate you. You have worked too hard, though, to allow your progress to end here. In a real sense, *The Confidence Course* begins when you lay this book aside and you live the principles you've embraced.

Let's review some of the ideas discussed in these pages. Then you will have an even better sense of how far you have come. To someone who hasn't made the effort, what follows are merely sound bites. A student of *The Confidence*

Course knows what the words mean and why some are emphasized:

THE CORE PRINCIPLES
OF *THE CONFIDENCE COURSE*

- Confidence is an attitude.
- Anxiety is an ally.
- Worry well.
- Understand what you fear; take action.
- Don't try—*do*.
- Courage is acting *with* fear.
- What is the worst thing that can happen?
- Compete *only* to improve yourself.
- True confidence comes from being accepted as we really are.
- What I am; what I have; what I seem to be.
- Children learn when to trust; adolescents search for identity; adults see beyond themselves.
- Put the other person at ease.
- We *need* to make mistakes.
- You are not your mistake.
- Success is a string of failed attempts to get it right.
- Focus on solutions.
- You *are* a storyteller.
- Pick a story for your audience; pick a story you like; practice your choice.

- Stories are everywhere.
- *You* are a story.
- Obstacles are an opportunity to gain confidence.
- Trouble and annoyance are not the same thing.
- We need to love.
- No one has the right to abuse you.
- To forgive is not to excuse.
- It is the relationship that has to be made ideal.
- The best way to help myself is to help someone else.
- Fix the image in your mind.
- I cannot control the world; I can control me.
- See your goal; sell your goal; *act as if.*
- Do not criticize what cannot be changed.
- What is it that I want but am afraid to reach for?
- A great talk needs anxiety.
- Research; organize; rehearse.
- Relax.

It is natural to want to feel we have control over our lives, that we have the freedom to *choose.* The quality of our lives, after all, is decided by the choices we make:

WHAT WE CAN CHOOSE

We can choose what we believe.
We can choose who we will become.
We can choose our dreams.
We can choose whether we will pursue those dreams.

221

We can choose our values.

We can choose what we learn.

We can choose how we learn.

We can choose what we wear, what we say, how we behave.

We can choose how much we allow others to influence us.

We can choose where we will be.

We can choose how we invest our time.

We can choose how we treat ourselves.

We can choose how we treat others.

We can choose how we respond when bad things happen.

Finally, we can choose to practice the Seven Steps to Self-Fulfillment:

SEVEN STEPS TO SELF-FULFILLMENT

1. **Know who is responsible.**

   Accept personal responsibility for your behavior. When you say, "I am responsible," you can build a new life, even a new world.

2. **Believe in something big.**

   Your life is worth a noble motive.

3. **Practice tolerance.**

   You will like yourself a lot more, and so will others.

4. **Be brave.**

   Remember, courage is acting *with* fear, not without it. If the challenge is important to you, you're supposed to be nervous.

5. **Love someone.**

   Because you should know joy.

6. **Be ambitious.**

   No single effort will solve all of your problems, achieve all of your dreams, or even be enough. To want to be more than we are is real and normal and healthy.

7. **Smile.**

   Because no one else can do this for you.

I have been in your head for a long time. You have been hearing my voice, weighing my suggestions, probably agreeing with some of my views and disputing others.

As you complete the course, I hope you feel that I have kept my word to you. I know I gave it my best.

My feelings at this moment can be found in a story I once heard a minister tell during a marriage ceremony:

Professional divers discovered a ship that had sunk centuries ago off the coast of Ireland. It produced great bounty. Among the valuables was a man's gold wedding ring. More than all the other treasures that the divers were able to bring to the surface, they were moved by the simple message engraved inside the band: "I have nothing more to give you."

Have a great adventure!

20

What Matters Most?

The Nobel laureate Elie Wiesel has been my friend and mentor for many years—and, as you would expect, I have learned much from this brilliant, compassionate man. One of the most valuable understandings I've gained from Elie was contained in a thoughtful reply to a question I once asked him about risk-taking: "We best prepare by building our inner strength," he said, "by sound philosophy, by reaching out to others, by asking ourselves: What matters most?"

Elie, of course, exemplifies the principles he encourages.

So does another teacher I know and respect: Kay Francis Toliver of Public School 72 in New York City. She has been teaching students in East Harlem since 1967.

Kay was "discovered" in 1992 by an entire nation when the Walt Disney Company presented her with an American Teacher Award as the "Outstanding Teacher of Mathematics" in the country. The following year, President Clinton honored Kay with another award for "excellence in science and mathematics teaching."

When I asked Kay to describe the greatest joy she has known, she said, "To see the smiles on my children's faces when they do something they said they could not do."

"I teach my students to be risk-takers," said Kay, who noted that many of her students face serious challenges. "And I teach them to have a solid center. I believe in the students. I know they can learn. But what is more important is that they believe. I work on that by celebrating their victories. One of my colleagues observed that my students always seem to be so excited. 'They are like that,' she said, 'because you are always excited.' Well, I am."

After all the attention she received in 1992 and 1993, Kay's classes were filmed for public television—and millions know her today from the programs *Good Morning, Miss Toliver, The Eddie Files,* and *The Kay Toliver Files.*

Yet, despite the exposure and the lure of other opportunities, Kay Toliver can be found on any school day where she has been since 1967—teaching at Public School 72. "I am a teacher," she told me. "I am proud to be called *teacher*. Teachers teach. I am where I belong, and I love it. I know who I am."

Kay's observations reminded me of the choices that Elie Wiesel told me he made for himself:

"I chose to be a writer and a teacher," he said. "We cannot live for the ifs—if *this* happened, if *that*, if I would have. . . . Each of us can make a difference. Personal happiness cannot be solitary. It must involve someone else, be it a girlfriend or a boyfriend, a husband or a wife or a child, a teacher or a student, a friend or some other person. We *need* each other."

What matters most to you?

My Most Rewarding Moment

Years ago, long after his death, I made a conscious decision to forgive my father. Although he was not alive to hear the words, I said them anyway. It wasn't important for my father to hear them; it was important for me to say them: *I had to let my anger go.*

Had I failed to free myself from my anger, I couldn't have grown larger. I could never have written the letter that follows. It is the reply I wrote after reading the words I shared with you in the Prologue—the letter from the teacher who had embarrassed me in front of the class when I was thirteen:

> *A few hours ago my thoughtful assistant, Gida Ingrassia, broke into a telephone conversation for the first time in the twelve years we've worked together.*
>
> *"Read this now!" she demanded, holding out a letter.*

"Now?" I asked, pointing to the telephone.

"Now!" she repeated herself, firmly.

I complied—and now I know that Gida was right. Your letter touched me deeply. It took great courage to write and to share so much of yourself. Your sensitive words bring my life full circle in the most beautiful way possible.

The title of my second book, The Greatest Risk of All, *has prompted several people to ask me, "Just what is the greatest risk of all?" I always answer the same way: "It is to be vulnerable, to allow others to see us as we really are."*

Well, you've taken the greatest of risks, and I could not be more moved.

The truth is, you were one of several people I hated when I was a child, and I added quite a few more names to my list as I became an adult. Painfully, I can remember times when my anger and hatred nearly consumed me. Not anymore.

I forgave you years ago. I even forgave me.

What I understand today is that you tried your best with all you had. I'm sure you blossomed in the classroom over the years and, undoubtedly, at a later time would have found a child like me a little easier to handle—but you should also recognize that you did teach me. You are my teacher. Just today you taught me again, about the extraordinary power of forgiveness. I was so moved by your candor and kindness that I called my friend Norman Vincent Peale, explained how you had seen the

article in Guideposts, *and I read your letter to him.*
  "Tell him the truth . . ." Norman advised me.
  "What's that?" I asked.
  ". . . that you love him."
  I do.

As you might expect, my former teacher wrote back—and, of course, Norman Vincent Peale wrote too: "This incident will ever be remembered by me as one of the most inspiring I have known."

I still struggle with the third of the Seven Steps to Self-Fulfillment—to be tolerant—but it helps sometimes when I remember what I've described here. I hope it helps you too.

LIST OF LISTS

Everyone's Fears	33
Two Steps to Worrying Well	36
Every Child's Three Questions	44
Six Ways to Have a Successful Conversation	46
The Three Phases of Adolescence	59
Three Ways We Know Ourselves	61
Six Steps to Overcoming Shyness	72
The Four SLIPs	79
RIP Mistakes	81
Three Fundamental Rules for Storytelling	110
Ten Ways to Move Beyond Anger	130
Are You My Friend?	143
Three Steps to Controlling Your Behavior	168
Six Ways to Comfort the Grieving	169
Six Steps to Giving Criticism	174
Four Steps to Taking Criticism	176
The Three Risks	183
Seven Steps to Taking Risks	194
Four Elements of Effective Talks	199
Five Secrets About Audiences	210
Seven Choices We Make Daily	218
The Core Principles of *The Confidence Course*	220
What We Can Choose	221

LIST OF CHALLENGES

Challenge #1: True Hope   23

Challenge #2: Not to Try   29

Challenge #3: Every Little Worry   37

Challenge #4: Appearance   42

Challenge #5: Make Someone Else Comfortable   49

Challenge #6: Join a Team   67

Challenge #7: Focus on Solutions   83

Challenge #8: Stories Ask Questions   96

Challenge #9: All Questions Are Good Questions   100

Challenge #10: Pause for Effect   114

Challenge #11: Envision   122

Challenge #12: Your Anger Log   137

Challenge #13: Cultivate Friendships   144

Challenge #14: See Yourself as You'd Like to Be   156

Challenge #15: Imagine a New You   163

Challenge #16: Act as If   165

Challenge #17: Comforting a Friend   171

Challenge #18: Goals   181

Challenge #19: Accepting Loss   184

Challenge #20: Risks   187

Challenge #21: The Choices We Make   217

AUTHOR'S NOTE

I'd like to thank Loretta Anderson, who, as my first editor, patiently read or listened to every version of every manuscript page I typed; Jack Scovil, my friend and agent, whose unqualified encouragement has been a life preserver on a storm-tossed sea; contributing editors Martin Timins, Lauren Picker, Anita Goss, and Eric C. Anderson, whose insights added immeasurably to the finished work; HarperCollins copy editor Victoria Mathews, production editor Christine Tanigawa, and interior page designer Joseph Rutt, for their thorough professionalism and unstinting attention to detail; my colleagues at *Parade* and at the New School for Social Research, for their suggestions and support during the two years I spent writing *The Confidence Course*; Marilyn and John Rosica, for their precious advice; all the generous people—friends—who are profiled or quoted in these pages, for their kindness and their wisdom; and the Horatio Alger Association of Distinguished Americans, for helpful technical and research assistance.

Finally, there is someone whose contribution to *The Confidence Course* is largest of all. He is Mitchell Ivers, and I am honored to call him my editor. Mitch created the final structure of this book, chapter by chapter, which he edited brilliantly. Truly, he improved the work—and made a friend.

ABOUT THE AUTHOR

WALTER ANDERSON has been editor of *Parade* magazine since June 1980. He is a member of the U.S. National Commission on Libraries and Information Sciences, and he serves on the boards of the Literacy Volunteers of America, the National Dropout Prevention Fund, Very Special Arts, the U.S. Naval Postgraduate School, and PBS.

He received the 1994 Horatio Alger Award, for which he was nominated by the late Norman Vincent Peale, and the Jewish National Fund's Tree of Life Award, which he received from Elie Wiesel.

He lives in White Plains, New York, with his wife, Loretta. They have two children.